Christianity

Rudolf Frieling was born in 1901 in Leipzig, Germany. He studied theology and philosophy and took his Ph.D. in Leipzig. He was among those who founded The Christian Community in 1922 and from 1960 until his death in 1986 he was its leader.

Among his works are *Christianity and Reincarnation; Hidden Treasures in the Psalms; Old Testament Studies* and *New Testament Studies.*

Rudolf Frieling

# Christianity and Islam

## A Battle for the True Image of Man

Floris Books

Translated by Hugh Latham

Originally published in German under the title *Christentum und Islam — der Geisteskampf um das Menschenbild* by Verlag Urachhaus in 1977. This translation first published by Floris Books in 1978. This reprint published in 1994.

British Library CIP Data

Frieling, Rudolf
Christianity and Islam.
1. Islam — Relations — Christianity
2. Christianity and other religions
I. Title
297      BP172

ISBN 0-903540-18-5

Printed in Great Britain
by Redwood Books, Trowbridge, Wilts

# Contents

# Acknowledgements

Unless otherwise stated, all quotations from the Bible are from the Revised Standard Version with kind permission of the National Council of the Churches of Christ. (New Testament © 1946, 1971; Old Testament © 1952). Italics in the quotations are the author's.

The quotations from the Koran are from Arthur Arberry, *The Koran Interpreted* (© George Allen & Unwin Ltd 1955) with permission from George Allen & Unwin Ltd. Those quotations marked 'Dawood' are from N. J. Dawood, *The Koran* (© N. J. Dawood, 1956, 1959, 1966, 1968, 1974) with permission of Penguin Books Ltd.

# Foreword

For a long time Islam was no longer taken seriously by Christians, but now it is again becoming a centre of interest. It displays a robust religious activity and is proving to be an important factor in current affairs. It moves forward with great self-confidence and one has the impression that many Christians are not equipped with comparable confidence in their own position. The spiritual foundations of Christianity, the divine wisdom spoken of by Paul (1Cor.2:7), who regarded himself as a steward 'of the mysteries of God' (1Cor.4:1), are threatening to vanish from consciousness. The basic doctrines of the Trinity and of Christ as God and Man have become for the most part incomprehensible dogmas which, in face of the prevailing materialism, people feel are no longer tenable.

A reorientation in the field of ideology is called for, a genuine 'expansion of consciousness' that allows recognition of the reality of the transcendental in a new way. The basis has been laid by Rudolf Steiner, the founder of Anthroposophy. This not only reveals the transcendental background of all phenomena, both inner and outer, but in addition identifies the 'Mystery of Golgotha' as the decisive, central event in the evolution of mankind and the universe. The profound wisdom contained in the dogmas is rediscovered and brought again to consciousness.

Only when Christianity is once again conscious of its own mysteries will it be able to face other religions and outlooks in a proper way—with deeper understanding and at the same time with the power of clear discrimination.

It has been the purpose of this book to achieve understanding on the one side and discrimination on the other with regard to Islam.

Stuttgart, Easter 1977                  Rudolf Frieling

For the numerous quotations of the Koran, the translator has used Arthur Arberry's translation, *The Koran Interpreted.* Where the author's meaning required a different translation, N. J. Dawood's *The Koran* has been used. Should the reader have difficulty in finding a quotation in another translation, he is advised to search in the immediate neighbourhood, as the verse numbering is not standard, and varies a little between different translations.

# I

# The Old Testament Prelude Abraham and the Theme of the Son

## The Great Promise

The Bible and the Koran are in complete agreement in attributing particular importance to the figure of Abraham.

After describing the creation and early history in its opening chapters, Genesis narrows its view, which initially focused universally on all mankind, to the history of the people of Israel. At the beginning stands the Patriarch Abraham, some 2,000 years B.C. A divine call causes him to migrate from Chaldea. 'Go from your country and your kindred and your father's house to the land that I will show you' (Gen.12:1). This removal from his former home was compensated by a great promise of the future: 'And I will make of you a great nation, and I will bless you, and make your name great, so that you will be a blessing. I will bless those who bless you, and him who curses you I will curse; and by you all the families of the earth shall bless themselves' (Gen.12:2–3). The promise turns into a blessing—which points again to the universal, to the mass of humanity, beyond any individual people, and beyond, too, the people of Israel that is to begin with Abraham. The real history of salvation starts with the call to Abraham.

The New Testament sees this history of salvation reach its goal in Jesus Christ. The Chosen People, singled out from the rest of mankind, has the unique task of preparing the incarnation of the great Saviour as a man on earth. Once that has taken place the salvation revealed can spread to all mankind. The Saviour is 'Son of Man', but as far as his earthly body was concerned he was 'Son of Abraham'. That is written in the first verse of the first chapter of Matthew's Gospel, on the first page of the New Testament.

Muhammad, who founded Islam 600 years after the appearance of Christ, himself looked back over the two and a half thousand years in which both Judaism and Christianity had arisen and felt that he was linked with Abraham. In the 3rd Sura of the Koran one reads: 'Surely the people standing closest to Abraham are those who followed him, and this Prophet [Muhammad], and those who believe' (3:61). 'Abraham in truth was not a Jew, neither a Christian; but he was a Muslim [one who surrenders to God] and one of pure faith [*hanif*—pure monotheist]' (3:60). 'The Torah [the Law of Moses] was not sent down, neither the Gospel, but after him' (3:58). Muhammad wished to recreate in its original state, the pure, early form of monotheism as he saw it embodied in Abraham.

In Mecca there was a tradition that Ishmael, Abraham's son by the Egyptian maid, Hagar, made his way to Arabia. The tribe to which Muhammad belonged traced its own origin back to Ishmael. In the 22nd Sura of the Koran, 'revealed in Mecca', the people of Mecca are addressed: 'He [Allah] has chosen you, and has laid on you no impediment in your religion, being the creed of your father Abraham' (22:77). Both the Bible and the Koran look back to Abraham. But the line of descent of Islam runs from Abraham through Ishmael to Muhammad, while that of the biblical story of salvation runs from Abraham through Isaac to Jesus of Nazareth. The elements Christianity and Islam have in common and those

12

that differentiate them appear in their original form already in Genesis. By following the 'phenomena' accurately, the following pages attempt an exposition of these original elements.

# The Time of Waiting

In silent obedience the seventy-five-year-old Abraham followed God's call and set out on his wanderings, trusting to the promise of the future. This trust was put to a severe test, for the promise concerned his descendants, and, as Genesis mentions, when Abraham set out, his wife Sarai—later called Sarah—was barren. 'She had no child.' (Gen.11:30). That is a theme which one meets time and again in both the Old and the New Testament. We know it in fairy tales as well. It appears precisely where the awaited birth of an important person eventually occurs. So it was in the case of Samson (Judg.13:2), of Samuel (1 Sam.1:2), of John the Baptist (Luke 1:7). It is precisely because of the painful emptiness of the preceding period of waiting that such births have their special quality. They are raised above the natural and everyday world of human reproduction to archetypal significance. In Abraham's case the paradox should be noticed that although his name already meant 'father', he had nevertheless to go without the son who would really entitle him to be called 'father'. The name 'Ab-ram', which he bore at first, means 'lofty father'; his later name 'Ab-raham' means 'father of a mighty host'. 'Ab' means 'father'.

How is the promise to be fulfilled if Abraham dies childless? This uncertainty and doubt weigh heavily on Abraham. The years go by. Then 'the word of the LORD came to Abram in a vision' to strengthen him (Gen.15:1). But Abraham's soul was now so burdened with care that he could not keep silent, even in the presence of a vision of God—'for I continue childless . . .

thou hast given me no offspring' (Gen.15:2,3). Thereupon his experience of God is enhanced. Genesis relates in its simple, vivid language that 'he brought him outside'; God led him out of the confinement of his tent into the open air and pointed out the night sky with its stars. ' "So shall your descendants be." And he believed the LORD; and he reckoned it to him as righteousness' (Gen.15:5–6). This is the first time that the word 'believe' occurs in the Bible. In Hebrew it is the same word as 'amen'. Gazing at the stars, Abraham, as it were, says 'amen' with his whole being, he lives 'amen', he confirms with complete trust the spiritual reality experienced. This is followed by a further increase in the significance of events by the covenant of the Lord with Abraham.

But Sarah remains as barren as before. And there is something deeply human in the fact that even an Abraham could not stay at the high point of his experience. He lapses into disbelief, and he agrees with a suggestion of his wife that he should to a certain extent help the fulfilment of the divine promise. Sarah brings her maid Hagar to him and, according to the ideas of the time, she is to bear a child, acting as substitute for her mistress. Ten years have passed since the migration out of Chaldea. Abraham does not want to wait any longer. The Egyptian maid becomes pregnant. She is arrogant to her mistress and eventually flees into the desert. By a spring of water the 'angel of the LORD' appears to her, and orders her to return, telling her, however, that she will have a son whom she is to call Ishmael and that he will have many descendants. 'And Hagar bore Abram a son; and Abram called the name of his son, whom Hagar bore, Ishmael' (Gen.16:15). The angel spoke of so many descendants 'that they cannot be numbered for multitude' (Gen.16:10), but was silent about a blessing for 'all the families of the earth' (Gen.12:3). The promise of salvation did not pass from Abraham to Ishmael. It was still unfulfilled.

Again thirteen years run by, until Abraham is once more granted a divine vision. Now the name 'Abram' is changed to 'Abraham', and 'Sarai' to 'Sarah' (Princess). Sarah is expressly singled out as the rightful mother of the right son, who has not yet been born. He is to be given the name of Isaac. 'I will establish my covenant with him as an everlasting covenant for his descendants after him' (Gen.17:19). The son is to be born at the same season in the following year.

# The Visit of the Three Men by the Oaks of Mamre

For a long time Abraham settled by the oaks of Mamre at Hebron 'and there he built an altar to the LORD' (Gen.13:18). Previously he had built a similar altar at Shechem, by the oak of Moreh (Gen.12:6,7), and then at Bethel (Gen.12:8). This is certainly not a question of accidental localities, but of places where transcendental experiences had previously occurred, and which had a particular quality. Hebron, with the oaks of Mamre, was just such a place with an aura of mystery. One can perhaps see in Mamre, the owner of the oaks, the guardian of this local tradition. This Mamre had two brothers, Eshcol and Aner, and Abraham was an ally of the three brothers (Gen.14:13). The three brothers of the oaks of Mamre may well have been a priestly brotherhood. The importance of the number three in the religious and cultic life of mankind is a very ancient phenomenon.

By the oaks of Mamre, soon after the vision of God which announced the coming birth of his son Isaac by Sarah a year later, Abraham experienced the mysterious visit of the 'three men' in the heat of the day. 'And the LORD appeared to him by the oaks of Mamre, as he sat at the door of his tent in the

heat of the day' (Gen.18:1). The original text leaves no doubt
that this was a transcendental visionary experience, despite the
naturalistic realism with which the reception of the guests is
described. At the beginning of the story the word 'see' plays
a noticeable part. The Lord 'appeared'—in the original text:
'he made himself visible'. Abraham *lifted up his eyes* and *looked*,
and *behold* (sees)—three men stood in front of him. When he
saw them, he ran to meet them . . .'. The three are suddenly
standing in front of him; he did not see them coming. Abraham
entertains them in the shade of the trees. They enquire after
Sarah and announce the birth of a son in the following year.

Theological commentators have time and again noticed in
this story the relationship, not apparently a simple one, between
the naming of 'the Lord' in the singular, and this striking threefold appearance. 'The LORD appeared . . .' but 'behold, three
men stood in front of him'. At first Abraham addresses 'the
Lord'—'My lord, if I have found favour in your [singular]
sight . . .' but then goes on to use the plural: 'and wash your
[plural] feet, and rest yourselves . . .' (Gen.18:3–4). Then *they*
speak: 'Do as you have said' (Gen.18:5). If this triad could be
understood in the sense that the Lord was accompanied by
two of his servants, by his angels, it would not then be possible
for 'they', the three and not the one, the Lord, to be the spokesmen. But it reads: 'So they said', and likewise after eating, 'they
said to him, "Where is Sarah, your wife?" ' (Gen.18:9). And
then the singular is used again: 'The LORD said, "I will surely
return to you . . ." ' (Gen.18:10), and the singular is used for
the rest of this passage.

An examination solely on the grounds of textual criticism
cannot avoid the conclusion that in this passage different
versions of the story have been carelessly put together. It
cannot be denied that in Genesis different versions have been
joined together. But deeper consideration of this text demon-

strates that some supervising wisdom must have worked with the editor who mixed the versions, just as in the first two chapters an Elohist and Jehovist story of creation follow one another. The economy with which the different names of God are managed makes good sense on further consideration. Similarly we must also credit the editor who has given us the 18th chapter of Genesis in its present form with having noticed the startling discrepancies between singular and plural and with having nevertheless let them stand, thanks to a higher inspiration. The shock can then provide the impetus for reading between the lines what is not expressed.

Early Christian theology thought that the mystery of the Trinity was foreshadowed in the Old Testament by the Mamre story. It was found also in those places where the deity speaks in the plural. 'Let us make man . . .' (Gen.1:26), 'the man has become like one of us' (Gen.3:22), 'Let us go down, and there confuse their language' (Gen.11:7), 'and who will go for us?' (Isa.6:8). Similarly, elements of the Trinity were found in the threefold blessing of Aaron (Num.6:24–26) and in the three repetitions of 'Holy' by the seraphim (Isa.6:3). Modern theology has rejected this as a childish and naïve line of reasoning. Indeed, one cannot attempt to prove the Trinity by using such passages in the Old Testament in the old manner. Nevertheless, passages such as these do show that the Old Testament is open to completion in the sense of the Trinity, as it first appears in the New Testament. The fact that blessing is mentioned three times in Psalm 67, and that Psalm 99 has 'Holy' repeated three times is not yet sufficiently appreciated, nor the widespread evidence of a partiality for the number three in the religious-cultic life of mankind. Indeed the question must be asked of how in the last analysis it comes about that the number of three plays such a part, not only in the sphere of religious cults but in all worldly and human knowledge too. The key importance

17

of trinitarian thinking has been demonstrated by Alfred Schütze* in his book about the nature of the Trinity. The fundamental importance of 'three' in all human experience is a reflection of the highest divine mystery. It is permissible to perceive such a reflection in the Mamre story. At the moment Abraham takes the first step towards his 'son', there is a distant flash from the ancient divine mystery. God is indeed, as our language says so beautifully, alone, that is to say 'all one'; he is unique, but he is not lonely; he lives in the community of love with the Son through the Holy Spirit.

The icon painters have time and again portrayed the entertainment of the three men by Abraham. They made no distinction between the Lord and two servants, but painted three angels of equal rank. They knew that the divine can be manifested by angelic beings. The Jewish tradition speaks of Michael, Gabriel and Raphael as the bearers of the divine revelation to Abraham. Even the archangels are portrayed in human form—similarly Daniel speaks of the 'man Gabriel' (Dan.9:21). If the 'three men' were not the Trinity as such, they were, however, a revelation of it through the forms of three archangels. For the spiritual world, it is true that, as Goethe says, 'the one can live and be active in the other'.

The oriental hospitality with which Abraham entertains his guests is portrayed with vivid realism. The deeper truth that is present here finds expression in the Revelation to John: 'I will come in to him and eat with him, and he with me' (Rev.3:20). 'And he with me'—that recognizes the partnership of man with God. It is part of the dignity of man that he is permitted, by the grace of God, to give something to God. Man's action on earth can be of importance to the higher world above him. The angels of Jacob's ladder do not only carry gifts down from heaven. As they climb up they carry on high what

* Alfred Schütze, *Vom Wesen der Trinität*.

18

man can offer from the realm of his own free individuality on earth. 'And he with me.'

It is in the spirit of this partnership that the Lord says: 'Shall I hide from Abraham, what I am about to do . . .?' (Gen.18:17). The problem is the imminent punishment of Sodom. 'The servant does not know what his master is doing' says the Gospel of John (15:15). Abraham is allowed to gain an insight into the divine intention, and he is allowed to intercede on behalf of the city if there are still a number of the righteous there.

In the discussion with Abraham we hear for the second time the great promise of salvation: 'all the nations of the earth shall bless themselves by him' (Gen.18:18).

With the birth of the son under the sign of the Three, the step is also taken which leads from the isolated Abraham to the triad of the patriarchs. 'The God of Abraham, Isaac and Jacob (Israel)'—this formulation, which appears at the high points of the Old Testament, is also an anticipation of the trinitarian experience of God. In the 48th chapter of Genesis, this form of God's name can be seen in the process of formation when Jacob gives his dying blessing.

The God before whom my fathers Abraham and Isaac walked,
the God who has led me all my life long to this day,
the angel who has redeemed from all evil, bless the lads;
And in them let my name be perpetuated, and the
    name of my fathers, Abraham and Isaac. (Gen.48:15–16)

On Sinai God reveals himself to Moses in the burning bush: 'I am the God of your father, the God of Abraham, the God of Isaac, and the God of Jacob' (Exod.3:6). Three times does Moses hear this threefold naming of God; after the first time (Exod.3:6), then a second time: 'Say this to the people of Israel, "The LORD, the God of your fathers, the God of Abraham, the God of Isaac, and the God of Jacob, has sent me to you" ' (Exod.3:15). And in similar words for the third time (Exod.3:16). This occurs again in Exodus 4:5. Elijah, when praying on Mount Carmel for fire to come down from heaven, cries: 'O LORD, God of Abraham, Isaac, and Israel . . .' (1Kings 18:36). Among the Kings we meet this formula with David and Hezekiah. In his farewell prayer David calls on 'the God of Abraham, Isaac, and Israel' (1Chron.29:18). Hezekiah invites the whole people after his reform of religious rites to a passover feast. 'So couriers went throughout all Israel and Judah with letters from the king and his princes, as the king had commanded, saying, "O people of Israel, return to the LORD, the God of Abraham, Isaac, and Israel" ' (2Chron.30:6).

This form of the name of God shows that a sensitivity to trinitarian forms existed in the Old Testament era, and is reflected in greater or lesser degree in these three patriarchs. In the New Testament we see the subject of the patriarchal trinity taken up by Christ himself. After the encounter with the centurion of Capernaum he speaks of the many who 'will come from east and west and sit at table with Abraham, Isaac, and Jacob' (Matt.8:11), and in argument with the Sadducees he cites what God said to Moses from the burning bush: 'I am the God of Abraham, and the God of Isaac, and the God of Jacob' (Matt.22:32).

## Isaac, the Son

The account in Genesis of Ishmael's birth is brief and factual. 'And Hagar bore Abram a son' (Gen.16:15). In Isaac's case, the report of his birth takes on the solemnity of a hymn. In the heightened speech of Hebrew poetry the sentences run antiphonally: 'The LORD visited Sarah as he had said, And the LORD did to Sarah as he had promised' (Gen.21:1). Isaac is *the* son. He is so called throughout Genesis, just as Abraham on the other hand is called 'father'. The fact that Abraham for his part is the son of Terah falls into the background; Abraham is a father figure. Isaac appears repeatedly as 'son', although he himself also becomes a father. Piously he gives the wells his father had dug the same names as his father had given them (Gen.26:18). Isaac is 'comforted after his mother's death' (Gen.24:67) by his marriage with Rebekah, a deeply human trait, which is characteristic of the pious son.

That Isaac is *the* son is most impressively revealed in the chapter on the sacrifice of Isaac. Gerhard von Rad,* in his subtle commentary on Genesis, calls it 'the most complete in form and the profoundest of all father stories'. In this account Isaac is described no less than three times as the 'only' son of Abraham. Right at the beginning: 'Take your son, your only son Isaac, whom you love' (Gen.22:2). The angel who intervenes at the last moment is the mouthpiece for a second speech by God to Abraham: 'for now I know that you fear God, seeing you have not withheld your son, your only son, from me' (Gen.22:12). After the sacrifice of the ram instead of his son, God speaks eventually a third time to Abraham through the angel with great intensity: in the Hebrew a word is used for this speaking by God which cannot be found anywhere else in Genesis, although it occurs in the books of the prophets, to describe an inspiration, a soft murmer of God. 'By myself I have sworn, says [murmers] the LORD, because you have done this, and have not withheld your son, your only son, I will indeed bless you, and I will multiply your descendants as the stars of heaven and as the sand which is on the seashore. And your descendants shall possess the gate of their enemies' (Gen.22:16–17). And for the third time is given the great promise of salvation, 'by your descendants shall all the nations

* Gerhard von Rad, *Das erste Buch Mose*, p. 203.

of the earth bless themselves' (Gen.22:18, previously in 12:3 and 18:18). To anticipate a little: this prophecy of universal salvation for all mankind, given three times to Abraham, is then given once each to Isaac (Gen.26:4) and to Jacob (Gen.28:14).

It is remarkable that in the story of the sacrifice Isaac is called the 'only son' with such emphasis. Is not Ishmael also Abraham's son? Not indeed the first born? And has he not also been given a promise of a great future? Was he not also loved by Abraham (Gen.17:18, 21:11), although Abraham at Sarah's instigation banished the maid Hagar and the 'mocking' Ishmael (A.V. Gen.21:9)? The sacrifice of Isaac is one of the most important archetypal images in the Old Testament. It throws light in the New Testament on Golgotha itself. Paul explains the Crucifixion with words from Genesis: 'He who did not spare his own Son but gave him up for us all . . .' (Rom.8:32). In his argument with Nicodemus, Christ explains his approaching sacrifice with the words: 'For God so loved the world that he gave his only Son' (John 3:16). Ishmael was Abraham's son in, as it were, the ordinary 'conventional' meaning of human procreation and he stood outside 'the story of salvation'. When a prophetic event of the greatest symbolic significance occurs with the offer to sacrifice Isaac, Ishmael, as it were, no longer counts. In this sequence of events only Isaac is present as *the* son. As 'only' son he is the forerunner of the *monogénés*, of the only begotten, of whom John's Gospel speaks (John 1:14,18; 3:16,18).

The sacrifice of Isaac is surrounded by the mystery of life and death. Even if Isaac does not die physically, he goes through something like an experience of death and resurrection, which is reflected in the Jewish sagas. The Letter to the Hebrews in the New Testament says of Abraham that when he was ready to offer up his son 'he considered that God was able to raise men even from the dead; hence, figuratively [*en parabolē*] speaking, he did receive him back' (Heb.11:19).

# Abraham in the New Testament

From the Gospels it can be seen how very much alive the figure of the patriarch remained in the consciousness of the Jewish people. Christ refers to this tradition when he calls the woman he has healed 'daughter of Abraham' (Luke 13:16) and the tax collector Zacchaeus 'a son of Abraham' (Luke 19:9). He describes from transcendental knowledge how in the life to come the patriarch is responsible as their spiritual keeper for the souls of dead Jews—in the parable of the rich man and the poor man, Lazarus (Luke 16:23–31).

At the same time, however, the great change in the relationship to Abraham which occurs because of Christ becomes clear in the New Testament. The evangelist Matthew, who rightly stands at the beginning of the New Testament as the link with the Old Testament, first of all looks back at the line of descent which has led from Abraham to Jesus, in order to deal with the great salvation 'for all the nations of the earth'. We have already remarked that he mentions Abraham by name in the first verse of his Gospel. 'The book of the genealogy of Jesus Christ, the son of David, the son of Abraham.' Then Matthew begins immediately with the family tree of Jesus, which, in contrast to Luke, he starts in the past, not indeed with Adam, but with Abraham. 'Abraham was the father of Isaac, and Isaac the father of Jacob', and so follows the whole list of succeeding generations which continually keep death in check, although it threatens to break the chain of generations, until they reach their goal in Jesus. It can be presumed that the variant reading, 'Joseph was the father of Jesus' (Matt.1:16), conforms to the original text, for otherwise the family tree would be pointless. The word *egénnesen* (he begat) is repeated with impressive monotony through the three times fourteen generations. This word disappears with the name of Jesus. That does not mean at all, however, that death has finally triumphed after two thousand years, sitting as it were, at the end of the long handle of a lever and making the 'die and be born' of the generations end in 'be born and die'. The unending procreation of the generations, thrusting death back, is carried on to a higher plane by the Mystery of Golgotha. Jesus does not overcome death by fathering a son. Because of the Christ dwelling within him it is a procreation, rather, of a risen body that is accomplished, which fundamentally changes the whole essence of mankind and which does not push death back, but rather robs death on the spot of all power. Here perhaps can be found the solution of the puzzle which Gottfried Richter* has pointed out. Why did Matthew, after speaking of three times fourteen generations, not give forty-two names, but only forty-one? Could the arithmetic of the tax collector Matthew have been so weak? 'Jesus' is given as the forty-first name. Instead of continuing 'Jesus was the father . . .', the Christ mystery of transubstantiation takes place in Jesus, and the forty-second name is therefore Christ. The sentence, 'and from the deportation to Babylon to the Christ fourteen generations' (Matt. 1:17), is then correct. The last generation is a *generatio*, a procreation of a higher order, by which the Risen One enters life.

This means that the line of descent from Abraham, till then a part of the story of salvation as preparation for the body of Jesus, now comes to an end, and the task of the chosen people

---

* Gottfried Richter, '*Von der Geburt Jesu Christi*' (*Die Christengemeinschaft*, Nov./Dec. 1949) and '*Von der Menschwerdung Christi*' (*Die Christengemeinschaft*, Jan. 1965).

is completed. In place of the chosen people there emerges Christendom, the 'Church', whose relationship to Christ is not dependent on earthly heredity, but has its being in the gradual taking in of his resurrection body.

The physical descent from Abraham loses its importance for the history of salvation. In the childhood chapters of Luke's Gospel it can be felt how pious people close to the births of John and Jesus became aware that the fulfilment of the promise to Abraham was near. This is so in the Magnificat of Mary (Luke 1:55) and in the hymn of Zechariah (Luke 1:73).

The change is clearly expressed by John the Baptist. 'And do not presume to say to yourselves, "We have Abraham as our father" ' (Matt.3:9).

The claim to descent from Abraham is argued against Christ at the autumn Feast of Tabernacles. The eighth chapter of the Gospel of John reports the decisive arguments and explanations that followed in answer. The events of the eighth day, which followed the seven days of the actual feast, are described. This was a day which was specially dedicated among the Jews of those days to the memory of Abraham. Obviously, precisely on this day the name of Abraham would be heard in Jerusalem. Christ spoke these words: 'the truth will make you free' (John 8:32). In reply came this objection: 'We are descendants of Abraham, and have never been in bondage to any one', and therefore in no need of liberation. The answer: 'I know that you are descendants of Abraham'. But he told them that in fact his words found no place in their souls, that they were even conspiring to kill him, and he explained to them that they were far from the true Abraham, despite their descent. Instead of Abraham, they were in reality evilly inspired by a quite different being. Abraham himself, as an individuality living on in the world of the spirit, 'rejoiced that he was to see my day' (John 8:56). With the breaking of this 'day' a new era has begun. Now it is time for man to find a way, without reference to his physical descent, of joining his ego with the higher ego of Christ. 'Before Abraham was, I am' (John 8:58). This great selfless 'I' is the Son. And transcending the example given by Isaac, Christ becomes THE SON in John's Gospel in the absolute sense. 'If the Son makes you free, you will be free indeed' (John 8:36). Matthew, who at first describes Jesus of Nazareth according to the flesh as 'son of Abraham', portrays how in the course of his ministry Christ is gradually recognized as Son of the eternal God (Matt.14:33; 16:16; 27:54). The absolute expression THE SON also occurs in the synoptic Gospels, although less frequently than in the Gospel of John (Matt.11:27; 24:36; 28:19; Mark 13:32).

Paul sees the promise of many descendants given to Abraham as being fulfilled in future Christendom. Abraham is no longer considered the physical ancestor; for Paul he becomes the archetypal 'father of all who believe' (Rom.4:11,16), because of his trusting 'amen' to the divine promise when the Lord led him out of the confines of his tent and showed him the stars.

# Ishmael

Ishmael, the son of the maid, does not belong to the line of inheritance on which the great promise of salvation rests. With him a collateral line of Abraham's descendants is founded, which branches off at a time when Abraham had not yet found the fulfilment of his existence as true father of the right son. His name Abram is not yet broadened to Abraham, nor has he yet encountered the 'three men'. It is, as it were, an 'Abrahamism' not yet grown to full ripeness that branches off here, standing as a symbol of prematurity.

# Ishmael

Ishmael, too, as Abraham's offspring shares in the divine blessing and promise. This is not changed by the unpleasant but human exchanges between Sarah and Hagar, nor by the banishment (Gen.16:4,6; 21:10).

When the angel of the Lord finds the fleeing, pregnant Hagar by the spring in the desert, he prophesies to her: 'I will so greatly multiply your descendants that they cannot be numbered for multitude' (Gen.16:10). When the ninety-nine-year-old Abraham is told of the birth of Isaac, something which at first seemed beyond his power to achieve, he intercedes nevertheless on behalf of the son he has had by Hagar for thirteen years: 'Oh that Ishmael might live in thy sight!' (Gen.17:18). At first the Lord answers him by saying that Sarah shall bear him a son, whose name is to be Isaac. 'I will establish my covenant with him as an everlasting covenant'. Then, however, he continues: 'As for Ishmael, I have heard you; behold, I will bless him and make him fruitful and multiply him exceedingly; he shall be the father of twelve princes, and I will make him a great nation' (Gen.17:20). When later on, after their banishment, Hagar and her son were close to dying of thirst in the wilderness, the angel showed her the spring and saved them. The threatened life of Ishmael was safeguarded by divine intervention.

Ishmael appears once more in the Genesis account at the death of Abraham. Despite the previous separation, 'Isaac and Ishmael his sons buried him' (Gen.25:9). Genesis then adds a list of Ishmael's descendants, naming the twelve princes descended from him, some of whom at least unmistakably point to Arabia, for instance Kedar, Dumah, Massa, Tema (Gen.25:13-15). It is clear that Ishmael's descendants in Arabia joined the semitic Joktanites, who were already living there, according to the list of nations in Genesis 10:25.

The account in Genesis gives the impression that the

Ishmaelite collateral line of Abraham's descendants was involved in the far-reaching plans of divine providence, even though standing outside the great promise of salvation. Although a collateral line, it is nevertheless also an 'Abrahamism'. When Abraham sent Hagar and her son away against his own will, the voice of God said to him: 'And I will make a nation of the son of the slave woman also, because he is your offspring' (Gen.21:13).

In the end the line of Abraham and Isaac leads to Jerusalem, the line of Abraham and Ishmael to Mecca.

# II
# Muhammad

## His Beginnings

In the Koran, Mecca is called 'The Mother of Cities' (6:92, 42:5). From the earliest times it was a holy city for the Arabs, above all because of the Kaaba. This word means a cube, or a dice. A black meteorite had been built into the wall of a rectangular building. Certain months of the year were set apart as a time of inviolable peace of God for the pilgrimage to Mecca. The pilgrimage followed a prescribed ritual whose climax was the walking seven times round the Kaaba. This had to be done anti-clockwise, as in this way the heart was turned to the inner side of the circle. In making this circuit, the pilgrims kissed the black stone. As well as being important as a goal of pilgrimage, Mecca was also important as a commercial city. Here converged the caravan routes which led to southern Arabia, to Syria and to Mesopotamia. Every summer a large caravan set out for the north, and a similarly large caravan set out every winter for the south.

In about the year 570 Muhammad was born in Mecca, a member of the tribe of Quraysh, which, as already mentioned, traced its origin back to Abraham's son Ishmael. As a young boy he lost his parents, and was brought up by relations. When he was twenty-five he married Khadija, the widow of a rich merchant in whose service he had already proved himself as a leader of a caravan. This woman was very important to him, and he lived with her in monogamous marriage until her death in 620.

In about 610 the forty-year-old Muhammad had his decisive experience of religious calling. For some time before, he had liked to withdraw into the mountains for quiet contemplation, and it was on Mount Hirā that an angel appeared to him and holding heavenly writing before his eyes ordered him: 'Read!'. This, his first inspiration, is probably preserved in the opening verses of Sura 96: 'Recite: In the Name of thy Lord who created, created Man of a blood-clot. Recite: And thy Lord is the Most Generous, who taught by the Pen, taught Man that he knew not.' Greatly moved, he fled to Khadija, and she talked him out of his feeling that he might have fallen victim to an approach by the devil. When subsequently doubts returned, she talked him out of them and strengthened his consciousness of having a mission. Initially, Muhammad was not uncritical. He was aware that inspiration could come from another source than God. In the 22nd Sura Allah says: 'We sent not ever any Messenger or Prophet before thee, but that Satan cast into his fancy, when he was fancying; but God annuls what Satan casts . . .' (22:51). 'Indeed they were near to seducing thee from what We revealed to thee, that thou mightest forge against Us another . . .' (17:75). Once he proclaimed as a saying of God an endorsement of the worship, customary in Mecca, of the three female divinities known as 'Allah's Daughters': 'These are the high flying swans for whose intercession men pray'. Nevertheless he had to acknowledge to himself that with this saying he was grossly betraying his strict monotheism. Accordingly on the following day he declared this passage to be inspired by Satan, and although this attracted fresh hostility, he replaced the passage with an orthodox text (53:19,20).

It is said that Muhammad 'composed' his suras himself, an assertion which he always rejected. 'Or do they say, "He has forged it [the Koran]"? Say: "Then bring you ten suras the like of it, forged;" ' (11:16 also 52:33). He does not want to hear about 'poets'. The concept 'poet' had a special connotation in Arabia at that time. A passage from Frants Buhl's life of Muhammad may be quoted here: 'Arabian poetry in Muhammad's time had a long history of development behind it . . . But it is still more important, as Goldziher has shown in one of his admirable essays, that the poets developed from the old soothsayers, and many of their characteristics can be understood only if they are seen as an inheritance from their predecessors. Even the word poet, shā'ir, "he who knows", points in this direction and also the fact that the old poets just as much as the soothsayers (kāhin) were considered to be under the influence of the jinn. Accordingly their advice was sought before journeys and battles. One of the most important duties of the poets of old was to support their tribe by hurling curses at the enemy, for their tongues were thought to have greater force in this than the tongues of others. When poets in the modern sense developed from the old soothsayers, biting satirical verses replaced the original curses; but they still betrayed their origin and descent by being recited when various highly specialized symbolical rites were solemnized'.*

It clearly follows that the history of Arabian poetry is also the story of a development of consciousness. Originally all poetry came from a condition of heightened consciousness, from inspiration by supernatural beings. The muse that inspired Homer was a reality. In ancient Arabia there were the jinn, spiritual beings, that could speak through the poet. But in Muhammad's time the old clairvoyance and sensitivity to inspiration had already completely decayed. The 'twilight of the gods' had possibly arrived in Arabia much earlier than it did in northern Europe. Equally, belief in life after death had already died out, although in ancient Arabia people had still

* Frants Buhl, *Das Leben Muhammeds*, p. 60f.

cried out to the dead, 'Go not far!'* The religion of the old
gods was utterly decadent. Muhammad therefore did not wish
to be confused with the 'poets', who were the late born offspring of a vanished spirituality. Among the phenomena that
accompanied this decadence was the appearance of lower
spiritual beings in the place of the retreating ancient gods, and
the appearance of men who were 'possessed', instead of
divinely inspired. Through those 'possessed', evil occult
consequences could occur.

It is from this standpoint that Muhammad's rejection is to
be understood. 'Shall I tell you on whom the Satans come
down? They come down on every guilty impostor. They give
ear, but most of them are liars. And the poets—the perverse
follow them; hast thou not seen how they wander in every
valley and how they say that which they do not?' (26:221–225).
'Nay, but they say: "A hotchpotch of nightmares! Nay, he
[Muhammad] has forged it [the Koran]; nay, he is a poet!" '
(21:5). 'What, shall we forsake our Gods for a poet possessed?'
(37:35). Allah says to Muhammad: 'By thy Lord's blessing
thou art not a soothsayer neither possessed. Or do they say,
"He is a poet..." ' (52:30). 'It is the speech of a noble
Messenger. It is not the speech of a poet ... nor the speech of
a soothsayer' (69:40–42). In Arabic the word 'possessed' means
'possessed by the jinn' (ma-jnun). 'They say: "... thou art
assuredly possessed" ' (15:6. Also 37:35; 44:13; 52:29; 68:2;
81:22). The word meaning 'bewitched' is also used (ma-shur):
magical influences emanate from the possessed 'poets'. 'The
evildoers say, "You are only following a man bewitched!" '
(17:50; 25:9).

Consequently the imprecations uttered by such 'poets' were
credited with the power of a real occult curse. In ancient times
the inspired word was more than 'information', it was an

* F. Buhl, *Das Leben Muhammeds*, p. 90.

effective force for good or evil. An inspired blessing had actual substance, while a destructive force emanated from a curse inspired by demons. This was why Balak, king of the Moabites, summoned the magician Balaam when he saw the approach of the Israelites led by Moses. 'Come now, curse this people for me, . . . for I know that he whom you bless is blessed, and he whom you curse is cursed' (Num.22:6). It would be naïve rationalism no longer permissible these days to see nothing more in such things than mere superstition. Of these magical powers only decadent remains existed in Muhammad's time; nevertheless he still felt the 'poets' to be sinister. This explains his intense dislike of satirical verses, which for him were occult weapons, not just political ones. Later, when he had gained a position of power in Medina, a man and his wife were murdered there after the battle of Badr by the zealous followers of the Prophet because they had both 'written insulting poems attacking the faithful'.* When finally Muhammad was able to enter Mecca victoriously, he proclaimed a generous amnesty, but among the few people excluded from this amnesty were 'two girl singers who had sung insulting poems abusing him'.† The two girl singers were killed. A consequence accompanying Muhammad's triumph was that in the end the 'poets' too made their peace with him, and some even placed their art at his service. But this only happened towards the end of his life. The entire time before this the negative condemnation of the 'poets' was in force, and the Prophet wanted in no circumstances to be grouped with them. He declared emphatically that he had faithfully transmitted the Koran as it was given him. 'Move not thy tongue with it to hasten it; Ours it is to gather it, and to recite it. So, when We recite it, follow thou its recitation' (75:16–18). At first certain physical symptoms

* F. Buhl, *Das Leben Muhammeds*, p. 248.
† F. Buhl, *Das Leben Muhammeds*, p. 318.

frightened him when the moments of inspiration seized him. He had Khadija wrap him in a cloak at such times. Accordingly the early suras bear the title 'Enwrapped', because of beginning 'O thou enwrapped in thy robes' (73:1) and 'Shrouded', because of beginning 'O thou shrouded in thy mantle' (74:1). At this point it may perhaps be mentioned that the young Goethe, who had read a German translation of the Koran in Frankfurt in 1772, in 1773 wrote a draft of a play about Muhammad. The scene: 'Open country. Starry sky. Muhammad alone.' Halima, his foster mother, calls him, and warns him of the dangers of the night. He tries to tell her of his sole God. Halima: 'Where is his dwelling place?' Muhammad: 'Everywhere'. Halima: 'That means nowhere. Have you arms that can grasp him when he is so widely spread?' Muhammad: 'Stronger and more eager than these . . . and it is not long that I have been allowed to use them. I was like a child whom you wrap tightly in swaddling clothes, I felt arms and feet in this dark wrapping . . .'. Here the 'enwrapped' theme is given a deeper meaning by Goethe. This is assuredly connected with the letter he wrote from Naumburg on March 25, 1776 to Frau von Stein: 'How different it was ten years ago when I entered the posting house as a small, strange, wrapped up boy.'

Yet another idea emanating from the Koran can be found in this draft of a play, 'Muhammad'. He makes Muhammad say to Halima: 'How grateful I am to him [Allah], he has opened my breast and removed the hard shell from my heart so that I can feel his nearness.' Goethe had read in the Koran how Allah says to Muhammad: 'Did We not expand thy breast for thee and lift from thee thy burden, the burden that weighed down thy back? Did We not exalt thy fame? So truly with hardship comes ease . . .' (94:1–5). And in another passage: 'Whomsoever God desires to guide, He expands his breast to Islam' (6:125). Goethe responded to this very accurate image of 'expanding the breast', and this later influenced the second part of *Faust* where Hecate is invoked as 'expanding the breast'.

# The Preaching in the First Years

The first twelve years following his calling were a difficult time both for Muhammad and for the few followers he had at first in Mecca. The revelations which came to him at that time are not to be found at the beginning of the Koran, arranged more or less according to chronology, but for the most part towards the end of the book. The suras of these early days are distinguished by their brevity and partly by their highly poetic language. One feels that the Prophet must have been overcome as though by an elemental force. They are, as it were, forced out into short verse stanzas.

An important part was played by indications of the approach of the Day of Judgment. At the beginning of our era, John the Baptist was aware of the 'atmospheric pressure' of approaching global catastrophe when he cried out to his contemporaries, 'who warned you to flee from the wrath to come?' (Matt.3:7). People confronted with such awareness of the approach of the thunder of the Day of Judgment calm themselves for the most part with the thought that after all the world has always gone on and the prophets of doom must have been deceived. Today, however, towards the end of the twentieth century, it is certainly possible to think rather differently. The naïve belief in progress still dominant at the beginning of our century has been utterly destroyed. Does it not look as if mankind, released from every divine and natural law but incapable of escaping from the vicious circle of its own egoism, is heading towards self destruction and annihilation of the world? Isolated catastrophes are always merely symptoms, 'early warnings', which give a foretaste of what will eventually burst upon us. In the New Testament the apocalyptical consciousness of the possibility of the 'wrath to come' provides the dark background for awareness of the approach of Christ as the approach of a saviour. Early Christianity bore in it a certainty that nothing less was at stake than a *soteria*—a rescue on a world scale from unimaginable catastrophe.

Muhammad was unable to recognize this savour in Christ; he was well aware, however, that this earthly human world of ours was hastening to a great day of reckoning. In the twentieth century, for which Stefan Georg prophesied 'many disastrous defeats without honour', it can move us strangely to read in the 25th Sura: 'Nay, but they cry lies to the Hour [of judgment]; and We have prepared for him who cries lies to the Hour a Blaze. When it sees them from a far place, they shall hear its bubbling and sighing. And when they are cast, coupled in fetters, into a narrow place of that Fire, they will call out there for destruction. "Call not out today for one destruction, but call for many!" ' (25:12–15). One of the shortest apocalyptic suras bears the title 'Afternoon'. Outwardly the naming of the suras seems indeed for the most part to be accidental, yet connected to some striking word or theme. It is like someone wanting to call Goethe's *Faust* 'the book "*habe nun ach*" ', because Faust's monologue begins with these words. Similarly one sura, which has the title 'The Elephant', has nothing to do with elephants, and the long Second Sura 'The Cow' has nothing to do with the cow as such. At times, however, the title is nevertheless suitable in a deeper sense. This seems to be the case with 'Afternoon'. The 103rd Sura, which is the one concerned, begins with the statement, 'By the afternoon!' Some of the early suras begin with similar statements resembling oaths: 'By the white forenoon' (93), 'By the night' (92), 'By heaven and the night star!' (86), 'By the dawn' (89), 'By the sun and his morning brightness' (91). The Prophet feels a need to anchor his prophecy in the general human experience of undoubted cosmic realities. One might compare the passage in the Gospel of John where the first two disciples come to Jesus 'at about the tenth hour' (that is, about four in the afternoon), and ask, 'Where are you staying?' (1:39). It is clear that the sun has run its course and evening is inexorably approaching; it is time to look for a lodging where the night can be spent.

Similarly the 103rd Sura is characterized by lengthening shadows. The content is only an isolated cry, a sudden seizure by fear lest humanity be lost. The sura says: 'By the afternoon! Surely Man is in the way of loss, save those who believe, and do righteous deeds, and counsel each other unto the truth, and counsel each other to be steadfast.'

We can be equally struck today when the 102nd Sura singles out what drives humanity towards catastrophe—'worldly gain'. 'Your hearts are taken up with worldly gain from the cradle to the grave. But you shall know. You shall before long come to know. Indeed, if you knew the truth with certainty, you would see the fire of Hell: you would see it with your very eyes. Then, on that day, you shall be questioned about your joys' (102 Dawood).

Muhammad prophesied a penetrating and exhaustive Day of Judgment. Nothing will be forgotten. The earth itself, as a cosmic personal being, will give evidence of how the human being spent his earthly life, the good as well as the evil. The classical expression of this is in the 99th Sura, with the title 'The Earthquake': 'When earth is shaken with a mighty shaking and earth brings forth her burdens, and Man says, "What ails her?" upon that day she shall tell her tidings for that her Lord has inspired her. Upon that day men shall issue in scatterings to see their works, and whoso has done an atom's weight of good shall see it, and whoso has done an atom's weight of evil shall see it.'

The Judgment will treat each separate person quite individually. There no soul will be able to intercede for another. 'A day when no soul shall possess aught to succour another soul; that day the Command shall belong unto God' (82:19). On the Day of Judgment the soul will come upon the deeds it has done on earth as something that it has 'forwarded'. 'That is for what thy hands have forwarded' (22:10). 'Whatever good you shall forward to your souls' account, you shall find it with God . . .' (73:20). 'Upon the day when a man shall behold what his hands have forwarded, and the unbeliever shall say, "O would that I were dust!" ' (78:41 and see also 2:223; 5:83; 8:53; 89:25).

In the Koran's picture of the world there is no place for reincarnation. 'Till, when death comes to one of them, he says, "My Lord, return me; haply I shall do righteousness in that I forsook." Nay, it is but a word he speaks; and there, behind them [human beings], is a barrier until the day that they shall be raised up' (23:102).

As a result of the Day of Judgment mankind will 'march onwards from state to state' (84:20 Dawood). The imaginative pictures which to the seer portray this world to come are nevertheless in Muhammad's case imbued with a certain earthy materialism. He looks forward to the complete physical restoration of the earthly body which will then either enjoy the delights of paradise or suffer the torments of hell. Even John's Apocalypse portrays the 'completely different' of supersensible existence (which would otherwise be inexpressible) in earthly pictures, but these possess a transparent quality and allow one to look at the supersensible as it were through a window. It is clear that the heavenly Jerusalem cannot be understood literally, materially. It is also noticeable that in the New Testament the imaginative portrayal of burning in fire as the condition of being damned never goes so far as to present this in a grossly material way. In the Koran this particular boundary is frequently crossed, for example in the 4th Sura: 'As often as their skins are wholly burned, We shall give them in exchange other skins, that they may taste the chastisement' (4:59). Or, when the damned drink 'boiling water like . . . thirsty camels' (56:54), 'that tears their bowels asunder' (47:17), or when they must drink 'boiling water and pus' (38:57). But untouched by such corruption of the imagination the references to the 'hour'—it is called 'the Clatterer' (101:1)—are marked by a sublime and profound solemnity.

The other principal theme is that of strict monotheistic confession of Allah as the one, sole, transcendent God, and the commemoration of his omnipotence and goodness made manifest in his creation, together with exhortation to gratitude and complete surrender—Abraham's pure monotheism in place of the paganism which speaks of many gods, or even allows Allah to have daughters.

Originally there was no such clear-cut distinction between monotheism and polytheism. From an inherited, instinctive clairvoyance mankind had, in definite and differentiated ways, experienced a rich spiritual world, and this experience included a greater or lesser sense of knowing that some last, loftiest peak must rule over the expanse of this mountainous landscape. Gradually, perception of these beings as palpably close was lost and the images of the gods lost their transparency. And in the place of these loftier beings which could no longer be perceived came demoniacal and spectral powers of a lower nature, which are indeed not unknown in the New Testament. Clearly the three daughters of Allah—Manāt, Uzzā and Allāt—who were

39

worshipped by the Arabs in those days, were originally higher jinn, spiritual beings whom people actively experienced in the various provinces of the soul's life. 'Daughters' of Allah should certainly not mean that Allah had begotten them with a woman in the human fashion. People felt that these spirit beings lay open to higher spheres, and they sensed a higher divinity working down through these jinn from above. They imagined them in the noble image of the high flying swans. In Muhammad's time all this had become decadent. Muhammad could not do justice to the dying embers of paganism's ancient revelations. He had therefore to treat the pagan gods as devils so that he might look upwards to the high peak of oneness. With the growing power of abstraction that emanated from his purely intellectual thinking, he grasped the 'one' God and concentrated all his religious feelings on him.

# The Jinn

Early Christian polemic facilely rejected Muhammad, with his claim to be a prophet, as a fraud. This he was certainly not. Unquestionably he had supersensible experiences and inspirations. The only questions are how contact was established in each individual case with the sources of these inspirations, what kind of spirit being spoke through him and which impurities from his own soul nature may have been intermingled.

An experience which we have no reason to doubt is the encounter with the jinn in the desert. It was towards the end of his difficult Mecca years, when he came forward in the town of Tāif and preached, but was completely rejected by the inhabitants, who adhered above all else to the 'Daughters of Allah'. After this failure, Muhammad spent some time in deep depression in the loneliness of the desert. His disturbed emotions may have helped to make him sensitive to the supersensible by a gentle loosening of the structure of his being. According to tradition, it was after the evening prayer in a valley between Tāif and Mecca that Muhammad suddenly realized as he recited a sura that he was no longer alone: a throng of jinn (or, as we should say, of elemental spirits having their being in a nature far removed from humanity) had assembled. The jinn listened to him devoutly as he bore witness to Allah. Clairvoyant perception of elemental spirits in nature has been frequently attested right up to the present day. Everything that is recounted in Celtic districts about the 'green folk' can, for instance, be considered. It is quite credible that elemental spirits should gather in that uninhabited Arabian valley with a kind of spiritual curiosity around Muhammad as he prayed and recited, even if the words which are written in the Koran as spoken by them may well have passed through Muhammad's consciousness and have acquired his phraseology. It may well be true that the spirits differ in their reaction to what reaches them from men. 'And some of us are the righteous, and some of us are otherwise' (72:11). The 72nd Sura, which has the title 'The Jinn', begins: 'Say: "It has been revealed to me that a company of the jinn gave ear, then they said, 'We have indeed heard a Koran wonderful'." ' Here 'Koran' does not mean the book, which at that time was still far from complete, but 'what is recited'. This incident is also mentioned in the 46th Sura: 'And when we turned to thee a company of jinn giving ear to the Koran, and when they were in its presence they said, "Be silent!" Then, when it was finished, they turned back to their people, warning. They said, "Our people, we have heard a Book that was sent down after Moses, confirming what was before it, guiding to the truth and to a straight path" ' (46:28,29).

In Christian Europe, too, there are traditions in both tale and legend of elemental spirits reacting in various positive or negative ways to what reaches them from human beings.

# The Night Journey

This evening encounter with spirits in the desert valley was soon followed towards the end of the Prophet's time in Mecca by a still more impressive supersensible experience, called the 'Night Journey'. He experienced being transported to Jerusalem, and from there ascending into heaven. There are only allusions to this in the Koran. The 17th Sura, which has the title 'The Night Journey', begins: 'Glory be to Him, who carried His servant by night from the Holy Mosque [the Kaaba] to the Further Mosque [the Temple in Jerusalem] the precincts of which We have blessed'. The other allusion occurs at the beginning of the 53rd Sura, called 'The Star'. 'By the Star when it plunges, your comrade [Muhammad] is not astray, neither errs, nor speaks he out of caprice. This [the Koran] is naught but a revelation revealed, taught him by one terrible in power [Gabriel], very strong; he stood poised, being on the higher horizon, then drew near and suspended hung, two bows'-length away, or nearer, then revealed to his servant that he revealed. His heart lies not of what he saw; what, will you dispute with him what he sees?' (53:1–12). Up to this point the words of this 53rd Sura refer to his vision of his vocation on Mount Hirā in the year 610. Looking to all parts of the horizon, he had the image everywhere before his eyes of the towering angelic form. The 53rd Sura reaches back to this basic visionary experience in order to establish alongside it the experience of the Night Journey, which is said to have taken place in the year 621, as equally true and valid. The text accordingly continues: 'Indeed, he [Muhammad] saw him [Gabriel] another time by the Lote-Tree of the Boundary nigh which is the garden of the Refuge [Allah's] when there covered the Lote-Tree that which covered [throngs of angels are meant]; his eye swerved not, nor swept astray. Indeed, he saw one of the greatest signs of his Lord' (53:13–18).

In the development of Islamic tradition the account of this Night Journey has been continually added to and developed and is weighed down by numerous details taken from ancient cosmology and mysticism. Nevertheless it is believed possible to single out certain features of the original happening.

When Muhammad announced in Mecca one morning that he had been to Jerusalem that night, and from there had gone to heaven, he met at first with the full sneers and ridicule of the unbelievers, and heads were shaken among his own people. Could such things be believed? This distant journey, was it a real miracle? It was only a dream perhaps? It can be clearly seen that a proper understanding of the nature of supersensible experience no longer existed. The doubts which had arisen among Muhammad's followers were eventually overcome by old Abu Bakr (he later succeeded Muhammad as his first caliph) vouching for the truth of the experience.

The story, which later on was continually expanded, begins at midnight with Gabriel's summons waking the Prophet as he slept in his house at Mecca. He was leading a white horse, whose eyes shone like the stars. The name of the horse was Al Burāq, 'the lightning'. The white horse is familiar to us in the Book of Revelation as an image of spiritually illumined intellectual power. Nietzsche once described a moment of inspiration in which he felt that he was struck by his thoughts as though by lightning. This white horse bore the Prophet through the air from Mecca to Jerusalem.

When the spiritual part of the human soul is strong enough,

or when the restraining force of the bodily shell is weak, there can be something like a 'getting out', a release before death from dependence on the body. There are well attested cases of this kind of 'exteriorization'. In the Old Testament the prophet Ezekiel, who was an exile in Babylon, declares: 'The hand of the Lord GOD fell there upon me. Then I beheld, and, lo, a form that had the appearance of a man; below what appeared to be his loins it was fire, and above his loins it was like the appearance of brightness, like gleaming bronze. He put forth the form of a hand, and took me by a lock of my head; and the Spirit lifted me up between earth and heaven, and brought me in visions of God to Jerusalem' (Ezek.8:1–3). While carried away he saw what was being done in Jerusalem. Afterwards he returned to his body which meanwhile had remained in Babylon. 'And the Spirit lifted me up and brought me in the vision by the Spirit of God into Chaldea, to the exiles' (Ezek.11:24).

When he arrived in Jerusalem at the Temple (which in any case for a long time had not physically existed there) Muhammad dismounted at the Temple entrance and encountered Abraham, Moses and Jesus. He prayed with them. Thereupon a ladder of light was let down from heaven which came to rest on the foundation stone of the Temple. With lightning speed the Prophet climbed up this ladder and straightaway entered the lowest, 'first' heaven which was entirely made of silver. Here, too, he found those essences which as 'group-souls' are assigned to animals on earth.

The ascent continued from one heaven to another, and their glory was exuberantly described. The description of the Guardian Angel of Heaven and Earth is remarkable. He was made of fire and snow, but the fire did not go out nor did the snow melt. 'Snow and fire', the loftiest purity and the most burning power of love, are there harmoniously combined.

# The Night Journey

This is assuredly a genuine vision. In the case of the other descriptions of these heavenly spheres, a certain deterioration in imaginative portrayal, such as we have already mentioned, is noticeable, and this time to the extent that the metaphorical is inorganically mixed up with the earthly intellect. The Arab genius has a gift for calculation. This mingles with the images and distorts them. In the seventh heaven, where Abraham lives, an angel is encountered who is larger than the whole earth. He has 70,000 heads, each of these heads has 70,000 mouths; again each mouth has 70,000 tongues and each of these tongues speaks 70,000 different languages in which increasing praise of Allah resounds. This is the principle of calculation degenerating and running wild. Such images, which simply cannot be comprehended, are truly 'not beautiful any more'. We do not want to place the blame for this excessive four times 70,000 on Muhammed himself; it may well be attributable to the account of his successors. In it, however, a certain characteristic of Islamic spirituality finds expression. A similar case of numbers running fantastically wild is found in the Koran. The 70th Sura calls Allah 'the Lord of the Stairways'. 'To Him the angels and the Spirit mount up in a day whereof the measure is fifty thousand years.' It is indeed not a partisan bias if one sees a more dignified statement, and one as it were in better spiritual taste, in the Biblical expression: 'that with the Lord one day is as a thousand years' (2Pet.3:8).

Even if the detailed portrayal of the seven heavens is attributed to the later writers, the seven heavens themselves occur repeatedly in the Koran. Muhammad still drew on the ancient cosmic wisdom. In the 2nd Sura: 'It is He who created for you all that is in the earth, then He lifted Himself to heaven and levelled them seven heavens' (2:27). The world too has seven spheres: 'It is God who created seven heavens, and of

45

earth their like' (65:12), 'who created seven heavens one upon another' (67:3). (Compare also 17:46; 23:17,88; 41:11; 71:14) The teaching is even found that heaven and earth were differentiated from an original single substance: 'Have not the unbelievers then beheld that the heavens and the earth were a mass all sewn up, and then We unstitched them and of water fashioned every living thing?' (21:31).

Muhammad advanced further to the 'lotus tree' he had mentioned in the 53rd Sura. Once more the description of this tree is an extravagant numerical phantasy. In the seventh heaven he also saw the archetype of the Kaaba, 'vertically above Mecca', and together with 70,000 angels he performed the ceremonial circuit round this 'House of Worship'.

Up to this point Gabriel was his guide. But Gabriel could not go beyond the seventh heaven, although Muhammad could. With 'the speed of thought' he traversed endless space, passing through two regions of blinding light and one of profound darkness. Emerging from this he perceived with reverend awe that he was in the presence of Allah and only 'two bows'-length from His throne'. Allah's countenance was hidden by 20,000 veils, for no one could endure his sight. With one hand Allah touched Muhammed's shoulder and with the other hand his breast. Muhammad felt icy cold penetrating his heart and his bones and then the feeling of cold suddenly turned into the sensation of ecstatic bliss.

Eventually he climbed back down the ladder of light and rode back home to Mecca on the white horse.

The widespread belief in a physical journey through the air is trapped in the superficial and material. The view, however, that it was just a dream does not match the experience either. It should be understood as a case of leaving the body, of greater extent than that loosening from the corporeal that always occurs in every sleep.

46

## The Night Journey

Tradition has handed down a small point of great interest. When Gabriel carried off the sleeping man to his night journey, his wing hit a water jug which began to fall, but Gabriel stopped it falling as he returned from this eventful journey. The period of time which elapsed between the beginning of the fall and its interception was enough to contain all that happened on the night journey. This account gives evidence of a sensitive feeling for the way supersensible experiences take place outside or above the earthly passage of time.

Gabriel, the guide of the journey to heaven, was also the angel who brought all the suras revealed to Muhammad. Gabriel 'it was that brought it [the Koran] down ... by the leave of God' (2:91). There is an old tradition, which is endorsed by Rudolf Steiner's spiritual research, that Gabriel is particularly connected with the spirituality of the moon, just as Michael is with the spirituality of the sun. Muhammad received his inspiration from the spiritual sphere of the moon. It is not necessary to assume that the being called Gabriel in the Koran must be identical with the Gabriel we know from the Gospel of Luke. The spiritual region of the moon is, however, indicated by the name of Gabriel.

# Medina

A year after this Night Journey, in 622, the hegira occurred, the migration to Medina. At Mecca, Muhammed increasingly came up against rejection and hostility. He had, however, been able to establish good relations with Yathrib, north of Mecca, where the people were more willing to recognize his mission. In 622, therefore, he moved his residence to Yathrib, which at that time was called Medina, which means 'the city'. His followers in Mecca joined him in this move.

At Medina he soon won a commanding position. The years of repression and persecution were over. Now he also became a worldly ruler who did not hesitate to make war, and in 624 he won the battle of Badr, a name which means 'full moon'. Eventually, after varied fortunes, he experienced in his sixtieth year the triumph of entering Mecca. There was no further resistance, and in 630 he was able with a great army to enter Mecca, which for him had always been the Holy City. He cleansed the Kaaba of idols and incorporated the existing pilgrimage, whose forms and practices derived from antiquity, into Islam, which had its central place in the Kaaba of Abraham and Ishmael (see p. 54). At the end of his life in 632 Muhammed saw that Islam had been established. Allah spoke: 'Today I have perfected your religion for you, and I have completed My blessing upon you, and I have approved Islam for your religion' (5:5). The 110th Sura also comes from this time of victories: 'When comes the help of God, and victory, and thou seest men entering God's religion in throngs'. Islam had become the religion of a now united Arabia. At Muhammad's death—he died in Medina on June 8, 632—the organized, concentrated power of Arabia was ready to enter upon a course of world conquest. This development had been completed within ten years. In Medina the Prophet had become a powerful political and military force.

This development is reflected in the Koran. The revelations recorded in the suras of Muhammad's early Mecca period give the impression of having poured forth from a soul which felt itself threatened by apocalyptic visions of the approaching Day of Judgment. For the most part they are very short. The early suras are actually placed at the end of the Koran, which is not at all chronologically arranged. With each sura, however, there is a statement whether it was revealed in Mecca or Medina. Rilke wrote in a letter from Ronda in Spain on December 17,

# Medina

1912: 'I am reading the Koran, and bit by bit for me it acquires a voice in which I am present with all my strength, like the air in an organ'. Rilke probably received this impression from the early Mecca suras in particular.

While Muhammad was still in Mecca, however, the suras gradually began to acquire a different character. They no longer give such an impression of being forced out by elemental power, but resemble religious homilies. Muhammad still felt that he was in accord with the original revelations which had been granted before him to the Jews and the Christians. However, he had read neither the Old nor the New Testament. At that time there were many Jews in Arabia who had settlements, to some extent as closed communities. Similarly, there were Christians, although of very different kinds. A number of Nestorians and Monophysites, who were persecuted in the Byzantine Empire, had migrated to Arabia, as well as adherents of Gnostic views. Knowledge of their beliefs Muhammad acquired orally, and it was a confused impression that he received. The Old Testament came to him partly in the form of Jewish myths, and about Jesus he heard legendary stories of his childhood from the apocryphal writings.

Biblical figures were woven into the suras. The entire, long 12th Sura with its 111 verses is a version of the story of Joseph derived from the Old Testament. He is not aware that he is relating what has come to him through hearsay; on the contrary his version claims to be directly inspired. Allah speaks to him: 'That which We have now revealed to you is secret history. You were not present when Joseph's brothers conceived their plans and schemed against him' (12:102 Dawood). Muhammad was 'not present', but he has not been informed by some secondary account; the story comes to him straight from Allah.

The story of Joseph is attractive even in the Koran version.

The heart of 'the old sheikh' Jacob, Joseph's father, was full of foreboding and he realized immediately that his sons were deceiving him when they showed him the bloodstained shirt of his darling, alleging that he had been mangled by a wolf. 'No, but your spirits tempted you to do somewhat' (12:18). 'I know from God that you know not' (12:86). Potiphar's wife 'desired him; and he would have taken her, but that he saw the proof of his Lord. So was it, that We [Allah] might turn away from him evil and abomination' (12:24). Potiphar's wife appears in a friendlier light than in Genesis. When Joseph is released from prison, the Governor's wife said, 'Now the truth is at last discovered; I solicited him; he is a truthful man' (12:51). When she was criticized by other women for seducing her servant she invited these women to a banquet, gave them sharp knives and then showed Joseph to them. When they saw him, they all cried out: 'God save us! This is no mortal; he is no other but a noble angel' (12:31). They were so captivated by his appearance that they were careless with the sharp knives and cut their hands. Thomas Mann included this passage from the Koran in his novel about Joseph. From the 12th Sura one gets an idea of how widely such stories were told at the resting places of caravans in the ancient Orient and how this led to various modifications. Later on Yusuf (Joseph) and Potiphar's wife, now called Zulaykha, were honoured as an ideal pair of lovers. In the fifteenth century the Persian poet, Jami, wrote the novel *Yusuf and Zulaykha*, Goethe included the names in his *West-Östlicher Divan*.

In Medina the suras became wider in their scope. They were by this time to a large extent publications of laws regulating with the authority of Allah the organization of the Islamic community down to the smallest detail. In Mecca Muhammad had been a witness to his faith who suffered persecution; in Medina he became a ruler and war leader. The use of force in Allah's service presented no further problem after the battle of Badr.

Concerning the murderer of a man who himself had committed no murder or any other act of violence in the country, this word of Allah applied: '[he] shall be as if he had slain mankind altogether, and whoso gives life to a soul, shall be as if he had given life to mankind altogether' (5:35). But there was no restraint at all to killing in war. 'Then, when the sacred months are drawn away, slay the idolaters wherever you find them' (9:5). 'When you meet the unbelievers, smite their necks, then, when you have made wide slaughter among them, tie fast the bonds' (47:4).

The wonderful saying 'No compulsion is there in religion' (2:257) did not apply to 'believers in idols', although on the other hand it benefited those 'unbelievers' who as Jews, Christians or Zoroastrians belonged to a 'book religion'. The toleration of the Arabian conquerors later put the Christian nations to shame. Whoever did not accept Islam had to pay a poll tax and as a second class citizen experienced certain restrictions and discrimination. But in comparison with the practice of Christian nations, Muhammad's toleration is admirable. Sura 33 shows how authoritarian was the attitude he adopted in Medina: 'It is not for any believer, man or woman, when God and His Messenger have decreed a matter, to have the choice in the affair. Whosoever disobeys God and His Messenger has gone astray into manifest error' (33:36).

# The Jews

In Medina, which in contrast to Mecca received the prophet so readily, there was a large Jewish population. Muhammad had had great hopes of them, since in his mission he did indeed preach the religion of Abraham and Moses. He was disappointed. When he presented his Bible stories he ran up against criticism. In the suras, Adam, Job, Abraham, Ishmael, Isaac, Lot, David, Solomon, Elijah, Elisha and Jonah appear, and even Moses. The Talmudic legends might seem familiar to the Jews, who could not, however, fail to notice certain departures from the Bible versions. For instance, Muhammad made the wicked Haman from the Book of Esther the Pharaoh's Vizier (28:5 and 40:38). The Egyptian Princess who rescues the infant Moses becomes Pharaoh's wife (28:8). Moses does not marry one of the seven but one of the two daughters of Jethro, and on the condition that he serves Jethro for eight years—Muhammad confuses him with Jacob. Mary and Elizabeth from Luke's account of the childhood of Jesus are joined with Moses and Aaron in one family, and Mary, the mother of Jesus, is treated as the same person as Miriam, the sister of Moses. At the end of the story of Joseph, Muhammad makes Joseph's 'parents' come to Egypt (12:100). A Jew who had read his Genesis would have to protest at this point that Joseph's mother, Rachel, had long since died and that Leah, too, by this time was already buried in Hebron (Gen.49:31).

Since Muhammad claimed the authority of Allah for his version of the Bible stories, he had no alternative, when the Jews with scorn and derision drew his attention to these inconsistencies, but to turn the tables and accuse the accusers, the Jews, and after that the Christians too, of falsifying their sacred texts. The Jews 'have perverted the words of the Scriptures and forgotten much of what they were enjoined' (5:13 Dawood). 'Hast thou not regarded those who were given a share of the Book purchasing error, and desiring that you should also err from the way? . . . Some of the Jews pervert words from their meanings . . .' (4:47,48). 'People of the Book! Why do you confound the truth with vanity and conceal the truth and that wittingly?' (3:64). Already in his Mecca period Muhammad had been instructed by Allah: 'Dispute not with the People of the Book save in the fairer manner, except for those of them that do wrong; and say "We believe in what has been sent down to us, and what has been sent down to you; our God and your God is One . . ." ' (29:45). All this was changed at Medina.

Muhammad saw the strong Jewish community in its compact settlement as a political and military threat to his position as ruler in Medina. Finally he made a military attack on them and eliminated them as a political power. The fate of the Banu Qurayza was particularly harsh. This Jewish tribe had conspired with Muhammad's enemies at Mecca. Seven hundred men of this ethnic group had to climb down into a mass grave that had been dug for them at Medina. The executions went on all through the day and continued by torchlight that night. The women and children were made slaves. This happened in 627. After the capture of the Jewish stronghold Khaybar, its commander was killed and his wife taken into Muhammad's harem. Another captured Jewess attempted to poison Muhammad. He escaped with his life, but had to endure the after-effects until his death.

# The Changing of the *Kiblah*

Connected with his disappointment that the Jews did not acknowledge him was the important change in the cult life of his followers which Muhammad introduced just two years after his migration to Medina.

The word *kiblah* means a 'direction' which one accepts. In the Koran it is said: 'Every man has his direction to which he turns' (2:143). At first, during the Mecca years, Muhammad had not yet firmly linked this spiritual experience of direction with the cult of a particular geographical direction. 'To God belong the East and the West; whithersoever you turn, there is the Face of God' (2:109). At the beginning of his time in Medina, while he still placed his hopes on the Jews living there, he decreed that his followers should turn towards Jerusalem to pray, as was the custom among the Jews.

This *kiblah* towards Jerusalem is found already in the Old Testament. King Solomon dedicated the Temple he had built and spoke a solemn prayer of dedication. In this prayer he said: 'If thy people go out to battle against their enemy, by whatever way thou shalt send them, and they pray to the LORD toward the city which thou hast chosen and the house which I have built for thy name, then hear thou in heaven their prayer and their supplication' (1Kings 8:44,45). It is said that in Babylonian captivity Daniel had windows in the upper chamber of his house 'open toward Jerusalem'. That is to say he observed the *kiblah* towards Jerusalem three times every day at his prayers (Dan.6:10).

In 624 Muhammad broke with this *kiblah* and introduced another. Henceforth the faithful are not to turn towards Jerusalem with its Temple but, with a total about turn from north to south, now to face Mecca with its Kaaba.

The Kaaba shrine with its black stone had from remote heathen antiquity been a place of pilgrimage for the Arabs. A tradition connected with Abraham and Ishmael had, however, attached itself to this place. There was a tradition that Ishmael and his father had built the Kaaba or, more precisely, had rebuilt it. The prototype is to be found in Paradise, where the angels singing praises pace round the House of Worship in solemn procession. Because of the Fall, Adam and Eve forfeited their sight of this. When Adam repented, a second Kaaba was created from clouds 'underneath' the heavenly prototype, but after Adam's death this was again removed from earthly sight. However, Adam's son, Seth, was later allowed to 'earth' the Kaaba and he built it in Mecca from solid stones, but it was destroyed in the Flood. Eventually Abraham and Ishmael built it on earth. The *maqam Ibrahim*, the 'place of Abraham' is indicated there, together with the footprint of the patriarch. Ishmael is then said to have married the daughter of the ruling prince, and by her to have had many descendants.*

From a historical point of view, it is highly unlikely that Abraham was ever in Mecca. But the possibility that the roving Ishmael found his way there cannot be excluded. In every case tradition points to a movement proceeding from Abraham and Ishmael into the Arabian world. In Sura 14, which was still revealed in Mecca, Abraham says to Allah: 'Our Lord, I have made some of my seed to dwell in a valley [the valley of Mecca] where there is no sown land by Thy Holy House' (14:40). 'And when we settled for Abraham the place of the House [Kaaba]: "Thou shalt not associate with Me anything. And do thou purify My House for those that shall go about it and those that stand, for those that bow and prostrate themselves" ' (22:27). In the Medina period Muhammad gave still greater emphasis to the Abraham–Ishmael tradition and its connection with Mecca. The Kaaba, and the worship of the Kaaba, was wholly identified with Abraham and Ishmael. 'We appointed the House [the Kaaba] to be a place of visitation for the people, and a sanctuary, and [Allah spoke]: "Take to yourselves Abraham's station for a place of prayer." And We made covenant with Abraham and Ishmael: "Purify My House for those that shall go about it and those that cleave to it, to those who bow and prostrate themselves" . . . And when Abraham, and Ishmael with him, raised up the foundations of

* Washington Irving, *Mahomet and his Successors*, p. 129.

the House: "Our Lord, receive this from us . . . and show us our holy rites" ' (2:119–122). ' "Therefore follow the creed of Abraham, a man of pure faith and no idolater." The first House established for the people was that at Bekka [another name for Mecca], a place holy, and a guidance to all beings. Therein are clear signs—the station of Abraham [his footprints] and whosoever enters it is in security. It is the duty of all men towards God to come to the House a pilgrim' (3:89–91).

The change in the *kiblah* in 624, the turning towards Mecca, aroused considerable unease in Medina at the time. 'The foolish will ask: "What has made them change their *qiblah*?" Say: "The east and the west are Allah's . . .". We decreed your former *qiblah* . . . We will make you turn towards a *qiblah* that will please you. Turn towards the Holy Mosque; wherever you be face towards it . . . But even if you gave them [the Jews] every proof they would not accept your *qiblah*, nor would you accept theirs" ' (2:142–145 Dawood). 'Whichever way you depart, face towards the Holy Mosque' (2:150 Dawood).

When in 630 Muhammad was at last able to enter Mecca as a conqueror, he cleansed the Kaaba, destroying all the images of the Gods remaining from pagan times; but he allowed the ancient pilgrimage rites to continue, which he established fully in the service of his religion. Mecca became the centre of Islam. The pilgrimage there belongs to the fundamental duties of a Muslim. Mecca may not be trodden by the feet of non-Muslims.

With the changed *kiblah*, Mecca was set in opposition to Jerusalem, and the Ishmael line of Abrahamism to the Isaac line.

In Medina, Friday with its public midday prayer in the mosque was introduced in opposition to the Sabbath and Sunday, but there were no other holiday observances (Sura 62:9).

# On the Question of Inspiration

When the apocalyptic colouring of the short suras of the early Mecca period is considered, there can be no doubt that it was as inspirations that they seized him with such power. To say that is not to decide from which region of the invisible world such inspirations came. As we saw, at the beginning it was for Muhammad no strange idea that one should test inspirations by testing the spirits (as in 1John 4:1). But with time he was imbued more and more with an uncritical conviction that he was the mouthpiece of Allah, and he claimed divine inspiration for each and every utterance he made, even those where primary religious feeling withdrew and the Prophet spoke as a law giver. Therefore when the sura in question comes to a decision which must have been very welcome to the Prophet, the genuineness of its inspiration is of course open to question. For example, by fighting, Muhammad's followers had desecrated a month always held to be most sacred; and then come these consoling words: 'They will question thee concerning the holy month, and fighting in it. Say: "Fighting in it is a heinous thing, but to bar from God's way, and disbelief in Him, and the Holy Mosque, and to expel its people from it—that is more heinous in God's sight; and persecution is more heinous than slaying" ' (2:213). On another occasion his men sinned against an Arab sacred rule by laying violent hands on palm trees in order to harm their enemies: 'Whatever palm trees you cut down, or left standing upon their roots, that was by God's leave, and that He might degrade the ungodly' (59:5).

Even if one may have no doubt of Muhammad's sincere subjective conviction of a genuine inspiration, one has nevertheless in many instances the impression that wishful thinking could unconsciously influence the relevant pronouncements. This is particularly the case with three suras concerned with domestic relations. After living in a monogamous marriage with Khadija, Muhammad proceeded when she died to establish a harem. This was partly, in accordance with the ideas of those times, a demonstration of what was now due to him as a ruling personality. Some marriages were concluded from political motives, others Muhammad entered into with powerful emotion. His personal and private problems could well be ignored if some of the marital problems that arose had not led to public statements in suras in the Koran, with its claim to divine authority.

In 626 Muhammad married the wife of his adopted son, Zayd. Zayd was devoted to his master and arranged his own divorce as soon as he realized what his master's wishes were. Contracting a marriage with the divorced woman gave offence, as marriage with the wife of an adopted son was considered to be incest. Thereupon the Prophet received a sura which decided in favour of his desires, and conceded his case to be an exception. Muhammad had concluded this marriage because it was the will of Allah: 'Allah's will must needs be done. No blame shall be attached to the Prophet for doing what is sanctioned for him by Allah' (33:38 Dawood). Further it is said: 'Prophet, We have made lawful to you the wives to whom you have granted dowries and the slave-girls whom Allah has given you as booty; the daughters of your paternal and maternal uncles and of your paternal and maternal aunts who fled with you; and the other women who gave themselves to you and whom you wished to take in marriage. This privilege is yours alone, being granted to no other believer' (33:50 Dawood). The faithful are allowed four wives, and there is no limitation of the number of slave-girls who can be taken as concubines. 'The Prophet has a greater claim on the faithful than they have on each other. His wives are their mothers' (33:6 Dawood) and as such his wives may not marry again after his death. The

# On the Question of Inspiration

33rd Sura considers the Prophet's jealousy, and also gives advice for the guests at a meal: 'O believers, enter not the houses of the Prophet, except leave is given you for a meal, without watching for its hour. But when you are invited, then enter; and when you have had the meal, disperse, neither lingering for idle talk; that is hurtful to the Prophet, and he is ashamed before you; but God is not ashamed before the truth. And when you ask his wives for any object, ask them from behind a curtain; that is cleaner for your hearts and theirs. It is not for you to hurt God's Messenger, neither to marry his wives after him, ever; surely that would be, in God's sight, a monstrous thing' (33:53).

At this time too another trouble arose. Suspicion of unfaithfulness fell on his favourite wife, Aisha. A sura revealed that she was innocent and directed that the accusers, as they were unable to produce four witnesses, should be punished with a hundred lashes (24:1–4).

Four years later one of his wives caught Muhammad, in her own quarters, with a Coptic slave girl, Mariya. This was not in accordance with the rules of the game. Muhammad promised to keep away from the slave-girl in future, but was released from this promise by a sura. 'Prophet, why do you prohibit that which Allah has made lawful to you . . .? Allah has given you absolution from such oaths' (66:1,2 Dawood). This last sentence refers to Sura 5: 'God will not take you to task for a slip in your oaths' (5:91).

# A Tragic and Fateful Rune

There is another strange happening which concerns this Coptic girl, Mariya. The Byzantine Christian Governor of Egypt—obviously a rather unusual Christian—had sent Muhammad, as a gift from a friendly neighbour, a white mule and two Coptic Christian slave girls. Muhammad's rise to power must have impressed him. The mule and one slave girl Muhammad sent on as a present to the poet, Hasan; the other girl, Mariya, he kept for himself and towards the end of his life she bore him the son he so ardently desired.

Despite his many wives, Muhammad had only two daughters, and no son. Khadija had borne Qasim and he had immediately given himself the title of 'Father of Qasim'—an indication of the importance to him of paternity. In Arabia it was shameful to have no son. But Qasim died in childhood, as did another son. And all through the long years until 630 it remained true: 'Muhammad has no son'. It must have been a 'trauma' for him. The strange 108th Sura refers, according to tradition, to someone who hated the Prophet and had mocked him as having no son when Qasim died, and so hurt him greatly. 'We have given you [Muhammad] abundance. Pray to your Lord and sacrifice to him. He that hates you shall remain childless' (108 Dawood). The word used for abundance was *al kauthar*, which is in particular the name of a stream in Paradise 'sweeter than honey, whiter than milk, cooler than snow.' The gift of such abundance was to compensate the Prophet, but the derision falls back on the mocker: 'He . . . shall remain childless'.

At last at the end of 630 the son of Mariya was born to the sixty-year-old man. The delighted father gave the boy the name which to him was the most venerable—he called him Ibrahim, that is to say, Abraham.

## A Tragic and Fateful Rune

But again fate intervened. At the end of January 632, at the beginning of the year of Muhammad's death, his son, Ibrahim, died at the age of fifteen months. He died during an eclipse of the sun, which can be traced as occurring on January 27, 632. Muhammad accepted this dreadful blow with deep and pious resignation.

It has the fascination of some mystic rune, this simultaneous extinguishing for Muhammad both of the sunlight and of a son's life.

# III
# 'Allah has no Son'

## The Prophet Jesus

Muhammad made the same criticism of the Christians as he had of the Jews: they had not preserved their holy scriptures faithfully. Allah spoke: 'And with those who say "We are Christians" We took compact; and they have forgotten a portion of that they were reminded of. So We have stirred up among them enmity and hatred' (5:17). It is humiliating for Christianity that an outsider like Muhammad received the impression that strife between the different schools of thought was characteristic. 'Yet the Sects are divided concerning Jesus' (19:38 Dawood). At times he had a better opinion of the Christians. The ascetic seriousness of individual anchorites appealed to him. 'Thou wilt surely find the most hostile of men to the believers are the Jews and the idolaters; and thou wilt surely find the nearest of them in love to the believers are those who say "We are Christians"; that, because some of them are priests and monks, and they wax not proud' (5:85). 'Yet they are not all alike; some of the People of the Book are a nation upstanding, that recite God's signs in the watches of the night, bowing themselves' (3:109) which could refer to the pious exercises of communities of monks. But then a feeling of their difference and opposition gains the upper hand, and the Christians are rejected along with the Jews: 'O believers, take not Jews and Christians as friends . . .' (5:56). 'The Jews say, "Ezra is the Son of God"; the Christians say, "The Messiah is the Son of God." That is the utterance of their mouths, conforming with the unbelievers before them. God assail them!

## The Prophet Jesus

How they are perverted! They have taken their rabbis and their monks as lords apart from God, and the Messiah, Mary's son . . . desiring to extinguish with their mouths God's light; and God refuses but to perfect His light, though the unbelievers be averse' (9:30–32).

These varying assessments of the Christians did not prevent Jesus being positively valued as a prophet throughout the Koran. The picture of Jesus given us by the evangelists is however scarcely discernible in the Koran; it is not recognizable through the veil of legendary and apocryphal features. For Muhammad every prophet was one who delivers a book. Moses brought the Torah, Jesus the Gospel, Muhammad—as the 'Seal of Prophets' (33:40)—the Koran, the authentic Book of God. The Gospel is therefore not the news of the descent of the Son of God and his redeeming act which changed the world, but rather the content of Jesus's teaching, which is basically the same as the message of all other prophets. A prophet is a messenger of joy, insofar as he promises the believers Paradise, and one who warns, insofar as he gives warning of Judgment and Hell. The kernel of his prophecy concerns the oneness of God, in the spirit of Abraham's pure monotheism. Jesus, too, is brought into this pattern. What else is said about him in particular in the Koran consists of legendary stories about his childhood, which at that time circulated widely in the Orient by word of mouth.

Sura 3 has the title, 'The House of Imran'. In this holy family Aaron and Miriam–Mary, Elizabeth, Zechariah and John the Baptist are found together. Mary and Miriam, Aaron's sister, are identical. Despite the laborious attempts at explanation by Muslim commentators, it can scarcely be denied that a gross anachronism has here slipped into the Koran. Imran, who appears here as the father of the Virgin Mary, is called Amram in the Old Testament. Exodus, the Second Book of Moses, mentions him in connection with the calling of Moses as belonging to the tribe of Levi. 'Amram took to wife Jochebed his father's sister and she bore him Aaron and Moses, the years of the life of Amram being one hundred and thirty-seven years' (Exod.6:20). The dumbness which struck Zechariah at the announcement of the birth of John the Baptist and which according to Luke's account lasted the entire time until the child's birth, is reduced in the Koran to three days (3:36, 19:11).

The annunciation to Mary runs as follows in the Koran: When the angels said, 'Mary, God gives thee good tidings of a Word from Him whose name is Messiah, Jesus, son of Mary; high honoured shall he be in this world and the next, near stationed to God. He shall speak to men in the cradle, and of age, and righteous he shall be.' 'Lord,' said Mary, 'How shall I have a son seeing no mortal has touched me?' 'Even so', God said, 'God creates what He will. When He decrees a thing He does but say to it "Be," and it is. And He will teach him the Book, the Wisdom, the Torah, the Gospel, to be a Messenger to the Children of Israel saying, "I have come to you with a sign from your Lord. I will create for you out of clay as the likeness of a bird; then I will breathe into it, and it will be a bird, by the leave of God. I will also heal the blind and the leper, and bring to life the dead, by the leave of God. I will inform you too of what things you eat, and what you treasure up in your houses. Surely in that is a sign for you, if you are believers. Likewise confirming the truth of the Torah that is before me, and to make lawful to you certain things that before were forbidden unto you".' . . . And when Jesus perceived their unbelief, he said, 'Who will be my helpers unto God?' The Apostles said, 'We will be helpers of God; we believe in God; witness thou our submission. Lord, we believe in that Thou hast sent down, and we follow the

Messenger. Inscribe us therefore with those who bear witness' (3:40-46).

Sura 19 bears the name 'Mary' (Miriam). It begins with the promise of the boy John to Zechariah and then turns to Mary:

When she withdrew from her people to an eastern place, and she took a veil apart from them; then We sent unto her Our Spirit that presented himself to her a man without fault. She said, 'I take refuge in the All-merciful from thee! If thou fearest God—' He said, 'I am but a messenger come from thy Lord, to give thee a boy most pure.' She said, 'How shall I have a son whom no mortal has touched, neither have I been unchaste?' He said, 'Even so thy Lord has said: "Easy is that for Me; and that We may appoint him a sign unto men and a mercy from Us; it is a thing decreed!"' (19:16-21).

That Mary gave her consent—'Behold, I am the handmaid of the Lord' (Luke 1:38)—is omitted in the Koran version. The birth is then described:

So she conceived him, and withdrew with him to a distant place. And the birth pangs surprised her by the trunk of the palm-tree. She said, 'I would I had died ere this, and become a thing forgotten!' But the one that was below her called to her, 'Nay, do not sorrow; see, thy Lord has set below thee a rivulet. Shake also to thee the palm trunk, and there shall come tumbling upon thee dates fresh and ripe. Eat therefore, and drink, and be comforted; and if thou shouldst see any mortal, say, "I have vowed to the All-merciful a fast, and today I will not speak to any man."' Then she brought the child to her folk carrying him; and they said, 'Mary, thou has surely committed a monstrous thing! Sister of Aaron, thy father was not a wicked man, nor was thy mother a woman unchaste.' Mary pointed to the child then; but they said, 'How shall

we speak to one who is still in the cradle, a little child?'
He said, 'Lo, I am God's servant; God has given me the
Book, and made me a Prophet. Blessed He has made me,
wherever I may be; and He has enjoined me to pray, and
to give the alms, so long as I live, and likewise to cherish
my mother; He has not made me arrogant, unprosperous.
Peace be upon me, the day I was born, and the day I die,
and the day I am raised up alive!' That is Jesus, son of
Mary, in word of truth, concerning which they are
doubting (19:22–35).

The child Jesus speaking in the cradle is found in the
apocryphal childhood gospel, *Evangelium infantiae salvatoris
arabicum*. When he was still lying in his cradle Jesus is said to
have spoken to his mother, Mary: 'I am Jesus, the Son of God,
the Word, whom thou hast born, as the angel Gabriel told you.
My Father has sent me to save the world' (Chapter 1).

Sura 5 is able to report a miraculous incident from the time
of the ministry of the adult prophet. The entire lengthy sura
takes its name from this incident—'The Table'. It could be a
case of a legendary reflection of the accounts of meals which
play an important role in the Gospels and already, by the way
in which they are characterized, lead towards the Last Supper.
The essence of Christianity is suggested in them, not just the
doctrine but, in the last analysis, the sharing of substance,
Communion. In the Koran, this reflection of the mystery
connected with meals takes the form of a legendary miracle:

'Jesus, son of Mary,' said the disciples, 'can Allah send
down to us from heaven a table spread with food?'

He replied: 'Have fear of Allah, if you are true
believers.'

'We wish to eat of it,' they said, 'so that we may
reassure our hearts and know that what you said to us is
true. and that we may be witnesses of it.'

'Lord,' said Jesus, the son of Mary, 'send to us from heaven a table spread with food, that it may mark a feast for us and for those that will come after us: a sign from You. Give us our sustenance; You are the best Giver.'

Allah replied: 'I am sending one to you. But whoever of you disbelieves hereafter shall be punished as no man has ever been punished' (5:112–115 Dawood).

Muhammad must have obtained his information about the death of Jesus from obscure sources, probably from circles practising a decadent Gnosticism. In the Gnosis of the first centuries, as far as can be discerned from the scanty surviving documentary fragments, there were evidently visionary descriptions of the actual spiritual spheres from which Christ descended to earth. This ancient school of spirituality found it difficult, however, to break through to an understanding of the tremendous fact that the one who had descended from realms of eternity into an earthly human body went through the experience of the death of a man on earth—that lay outside the scope of this Gnosis. It could not yet be seen that precisely through this death the God had so transformed his heavenly nature that it was able to become akin to mortal men and thereby able to enter him and join in communion with him.

An impression can still be gained from Paul's letters of how this real Christian mystery of a God enduring the experience of death was seen at first as something shocking, unworthy of God—'a stumbling block to Jews and folly to Gentiles' (1Cor.1:23). It was folly to the Arabs too. As Jesus was for him such an important prophet and in many respects distinguished above all others as God's messenger, Muhammad was unable to understand how Allah could let him meet such a dreadful end. So he clung to what reached him from the obscurities of Gnosticism. In Sura 3, which we have already mentioned (The House of Imran), it is said: 'They plotted', that is, the enemies of Jesus, who wished to bring about his death. But in opposition to their plans, Allah for his part formed a stratagem. The sura continues: 'and Allah plotted. Allah is the supreme Plotter. He said: "I am about to cause you to die and lift you up to Me. I shall take you away from the un-believers and exalt your followers above them till the Day of Resurrection. Then to Me you shall all return and I shall judge your disputes" ' (3:55 Dawood). Allah's plot in Muhammad's view seems to consist of snatching Jesus away from his captors, and smuggling another man into their hands whom they then crucify. In Gnostic circles there was a belief that the substitute who was crucified was Simon of Cyrene. The important passage in Sura 4 should be understood in this sense: Allah has sealed the Jews 'for their unbelief, and their uttering against Mary a mighty calumny, and for their saying, "We slew the Messiah, Jesus son of Mary, the Messenger of God"—yet they did not slay him, neither crucified him, only a likeness of that was shown to them' (4:156). It is tragic that Muhammad acquired only such an obscure conception of the Jesus–Christ phenomenon, one that bypasses the real mystery, and that the decisive point necessarily eluded him.

In this passage concerning Jesus, mention should also be made of the indication of the eschatological role of Jesus. 'He [Jesus] is a portent of the Hour of Doom' (43:61 Dawood). The 'Hour of Doom' is the end of the world with the Day of Judgment. Based on this statement in the Koran, Islamic theology has developed the concept of Jesus returning with the end of the world and playing an important part. In so doing Islam has gained something of the mystery of the Second Coming of Christ.

# Muhammad's Antichristian Thesis

It is quite astonishing that the Koran is able to say so much that is favourable about Jesus. The unique way in which he came into the world, the 'virgin birth', is accepted without question, and without anything similar being asserted about Muhammad. Jesus is called 'Word of God'. 'The Messiah, Jesus son of Mary, was only the Messenger of God, and His Word that He committed to Mary, and a Spirit from Him' (4:169). But 'Word' and 'Spirit' do not have the same weight as they have in New Testament Christology. Although he is called Logos of God in the Koran, the Messiah is nevertheless firmly placed on the side of the natural creation. 'Jesus is like Adam in the sight of Allah. He created him of dust and then said to him: "Be," and he was' (3:60 Dawood).

The decisive and fundamental Christian experience, however, is that Jesus Christ, although himself bearing the burden of being a man on earth 'like one of us', nevertheless in essence belonged to the other side, the side of God. When he entered Jerusalem on Palm Sunday the crowds saw in him the 'prophet Jesus from Nazareth of Galilee' (Matt.21:11). The rumour had already gone round among the people that in Jesus 'one of the prophets' had appeared. The woman of Samaria, who came to draw water, had already recognized Jesus as a prophet (John 4:19), and so had the man born blind whom he had healed. After the Feeding of the Five Thousand the Galileans saw in him 'the prophet who is to come into the world' (John 6:14). But the concept of 'prophet' is not adequate for the phenomenon which is presented to us in the Gospels. The prophets understand themselves to be authorized spokesmen of the deity. The prophetic formula ran: 'Thus says the Lord'. Not once did Jesus Christ introduce his sayings in this way. In the Sermon on the Mount he opposes his sovereign 'but I say to you' to what 'was said to the men of old'; not 'thus says the Lord', but rather the Lord himself speaks in the holy, calm composure of his divine 'I am', which is presented without any ecstatic exaggeration as a self-evident higher nature. A prophet? 'And behold, something greater than Jonah is here' (Matt.12:41). In the avowal at Caesarea Philippi, Peter utters the realization which 'flesh and blood has not revealed' to him: 'You are the Christ, the Son of the living God' (Matt.16:16). This avowal is the foundation of rock which supports the *'ecclesia'*, the Church, the future Christianized humanity. The Christ was experienced as proceeding directly from the primal Godhead. He had not in the first place brought a message; quite literally he had brought 'himself'. The 'take' of the Last Supper expresses his readiness to give his whole being to mankind. The passage through death and resurrection opens up the possibility of such imparting of himself to a humanity ready to receive him.

Muhammad could not perceive this essential characteristic of Christendom. The inflexibility of his particular monotheism stood in the way. He belonged to the line of descent which branched away from Abraham into Ishmael before the way into forms of trinity had opened for Abraham. Paradoxically, it could be said that Ishmael, although he was of Abraham's seed, continued the line of an Abraham who 'had no son'. In all the extensive recognition of the prophet Jesus, Muhammad opposed Christ being the Son of God with a passionate 'No'. 'And they say, "God has taken to Him a son." Glory be to Him! Nay!' (2:110).

The Koran repeatedly returns to this 'Nay!' 'They are unbelievers who say, "God is the Messiah, Mary's son." For the Messiah said, "Children of Israel, serve God, my Lord and your Lord. Verily whoso associates with God anything, God shall prohibit him entrance to Paradise"' (5:76). 'God is only

One God. Glory be to Him—that He should have a son!' (4:169). 'It is not for God to take a son unto Him' (19:36) With special emphasis: 'And they say, "The All-merciful has taken unto Himself a son." You have indeed advanced something hideous! The heavens are wellnigh rent of it and the earth split asunder, and the mountains wellnigh fall down crashing for that they have attributed to the All-merciful a son; and it behoves not the All-merciful to take a son' (19:91–93). The classical rejection of the 'son' is concentrated in quite a short sura which is sometimes given the title of 'The Cleansing'—cleansing from polytheism, cleansing from Christian belief in a Trinity. 'Say: "He is God, One, God, the Everlasting Refuge, who has not begotten, and has not been begotten, and equal to Him is not anyone" ' (112).

Therewith he also rejects the Trinity. Precisely in the passage already mentioned, where Muhammad uses the epithets 'Logos' and 'Spirit' with reference to Jesus and seems to approach the concept of trinity, it can be clearly understood that Muhammad did not realize the implication of these Christian expressions which he had acquired from hearsay. In this passage he immediately goes on: 'So believe in God and His Messengers, and say not, "Three" ' (4:168). Obviously his impression was that the Christians prayed to God, Jesus and Mary as three gods. 'And when God said, "O Jesus son of Mary, didst thou say unto men, 'Take me and my mother as gods, apart from God'?" He said, "To Thee be glory! It is not mine to say what I have no right to" ' (5:116). 'Who then shall overrule God in any way if He desires to destroy the Messiah, Mary's son, and his mother, and all those who are on earth?' (5:19). 'They are unbelievers who say, "God is the Third of Three" ' (5:77).

# Only a Dispute about Dogma?

These days one is inclined to question whether all this is not a meaningless wrangling about dogmas which we have long ago left behind us. Is it of any importance whether one sees in Christ the Son of God or not? The doctrine of the Trinity seems to many present-day Christians to be of no importance; they ask themselves privately whether preference should not be given to Islam with its monotheistic teaching so readily apprehensible by everyone.

It is quite true that the time for dogmas has passed. There should be a very clear idea, however, of what is meant by dogma. When there is talk of a dogma this refers to a certain type of statement, to 'How', and not immediately to 'What'. At the beginning of all religion there is a certain instinctive, primitive clairvoyant perception of the supersensible by a still youthful humanity. While consciousness of the material world and its inherent laws still slumbered, to a greater or lesser extent unawakened, the existence of spiritual beings was a direct, immediate experience. This situation slowly changed. The awakening of interest in the earthly world increased in brightness until it dazzled the ability to perceive the supersensible, and the 'twilight of the gods' began in a number of separate phases of development. In religious life people sought to retain what was becoming increasingly less directly evident to their sight. Finally there is laid down in 'dogma' what can no longer be actually experienced in detail, in order that the fundamental content of some former experience should not be lost. Dogma is allotted its place outside or above the other activities in man's search for knowledge, which have become rational. It can no longer be 'investigated', but must be accepted on authority. Dogma appeared more and more strange and incomprehensible beside the free experimentation of scientific thought and was felt to be a brake on progress. In the sixteenth century, Michael Servetus made an attack on the dogma of the Trinity, and had to pay for it with his life, because the teaching of the old Church about the Trinity still had unshakable authority for the reformer Calvin. Today there is an inclination quietly to put it aside without abolishing it.

If the modern tendency is now indeed to reject dogma, at the same time it may be said that, after the understandable revolt from dogma (insofar at any rate as it concerns the authoritarian imposition of 'How') it is even *more* in line with the times to put anew the question of 'What'. Modern man is pressing very hard against the boundaries of a consciousness that seeks to limit itself to the experience of the senses and the calculating intellect linked to the brain. This has shown itself in the long run inadequate for living. The real modern question is how consciousness can be extended, not in the sense of a descending into the uncontrolled subliminal but rather in the sense of rising to illumination. How can the lost provinces of human consciousness be reconquered while at the same time inner clarity and freedom are maintained? Rudolf Steiner's Anthroposophy has achieved the fundamental breakthrough to such a legitimate extension of consciousness in our century. New knowledge of supersensible reality has become possible. Because of this all those things which form part of the religious life also receive a new light. A task with a great future faces us: the task of gradually thawing out what, as primitive experience, had as it were been 'put on ice' and frozen in the old dogmas, and winning it anew for knowledge of a higher sort.

Lessing was in his own way aware of this task. It is remarkable how such a sharp-witted and clear thinker treated the dogma of the Trinity with respect, despite the powerful rationalism of the time. 'Perhaps this doctrine can bring the human mind, after endless mistaken wanderings to left and right, along the path to understanding that God to the mind, in which all finite things are *one*, could not possibly be *one*, as his unity must be a transcendental unity which does not exclude a kind of plurality.'* He explained in connection with thought processes of an earlier theology the extent to which it can be justified to speak of a 'son', whom God begat from eternity. In the same work he wrote the famous sentence: 'The development of truths of revelation into truths of reason is absolutely necessary if the human race can be helped by this' (§76).

What he describes as truths of reason should not be understood as meaning a superficial rationalism, but rather in 'reason' should be included what can enter the sphere of human 'understanding' by the cultivation of a higher, inner power of perception. Not that the essential wisdom crystallized in the dogmas could be grasped with a few shallow snatches of thought, but that reverentially cautious spiritual thinking may open up new ways of perceiving, along which mankind may sense his way into the great mysteries. The above-mentioned text of Lessing speaks very beautifully about bringing human perception 'on the way'. Dogma therefore is *behind* us insofar as it is a 'How', an authoritative injunction, but insofar as it is a 'What' it is *in front* of us, an appeal to perception. The statements about the 'Son' found in the New Testament are proffered as the pictorial expression of a powerfully experienced reality, which today has to be discovered afresh. In face of this picture, the objection of anthropomorphism is quickly raised — the projection of the earthly and human in a naïve, impermissible way into the divine. That is how Muhammad found the talk about a 'son of god'. He could not see through the window of this picture but remained caught in the all-too-human thought that if one believed that, then it followed that God must actually have had a 'female companion' with whom

* Gotthold Ephraim Lessing, *Die Erziehung des Menschengeschlechtes*, §73.

to beget a child as men do. It is also possible, however, to think that man for his part, as bearing God's image and likeness, may be called 'theo-morph'. Even if this likeness, this *'imago Dei'*, is marred in man, earthly humanity nevertheless gives some indication of the divine archetype. The Son faces the Father as an independent person. It is not a matter of a father's relationship with an infant. The Son facing the Father is an independent and free being. Today this type of relationship can still only be envisaged as concerned with opposition, as a situation of conflict. An archetypal relationship is sensed within the Trinity, a relationship in which Father and Son are closely bound to each other in the spirit of reciprocal recognition, understanding and love. In other words the statement that God has a son means that his unity is not 'exclusive', that from eternity it has been his nature to live with another free being in love and understanding and that his everlasting 'I' is not without an eternal 'Thou'.

# Consequences

When Muhammad denied that God had a son he confined him, as it were, in his absolute transcendence. This had consequences for man's understanding of himself. It is a definite note which is conspicuous and impossible to avoid hearing in the passages in the Koran about Allah having no son. The passage already quoted from Sura 19—'And they say: "The All-merciful has taken unto Himself a son." You have indeed advanced something hideous!'—ends with the words. 'None is there in the heavens and earth but he comes to the All-merciful as a servant' (19:91–94). In accordance with this it is said of the true believers: 'Thou seest them bowing, prostrating, seeking bounty from God and good pleasure. Their mark is on their faces, the trace of prostration' (48:29). Reverential worship is a part of every religion, but here this element is made prominent in a one-sided way. The 'mark of a believer' means the dust on his forehead. Allah, in whose presence there are only slaves lying in the dust, resembles an oriental despot, an all-powerful sultan, such as the world of Islam has uniquely and at times with some splendour produced. The lonely individual sitting on the throne can look down only on the backs of those lying in the dust; he has no 'Thou', no face-to-face encounter. Is he not in the last analysis poor, despite all his grandeur?

The inadequacy of this attitude is expressed in the Gospel of John, where Christ says to the Apostles: 'No longer do I call you slaves, for the slave does not know what his master is doing; but I have called you friends, for all that I have heard from my Father I have made known to you' (John 15:15 alternative reading). This accords with the relationship of Christ to the Father: 'For the Father loves the Son, and shows him all that he himself is doing' (John 5:20). This ability to face each other freely rests on their knowledge of each other.

When Jesus was asked by Allah (as related in the words of the Koran already cited from Sura 5) whether he had ever told mankind to place himself and his mother, Mary, as two gods alongside Allah, Jesus denied doing this in these words: 'To Thee be glory! It is not mine to say what I have no right to. If I indeed said it, Thou knowest it, knowing what is within my soul, and I know not what is within Thy soul; Thou knowest the things unseen' (5:116). 'I know not what is within Thy soul.' How differently Christ speaks in John's Gospel. As the light of the world he had opened the eyes of the man blind from his birth, and following that comes the passage about the good shepherd: 'I am the good shepherd; I know my own and my own know me, as the Father knows me and I know the Father' (John 10:14,15).

## Consequences

This free acknowledgement of each other by two people facing one another is also the pre-condition for true love. The old Fathers of the Church were on the right track when they endeavoured to use love to throw light on the mystery of the Trinity. If God is love (1John 4:8), then a 'Thou' goes with his 'I', and that indeed from eternity, not just from the creation of the world. Again, this too can be read in John's Gospel. In the prayer which is sometimes called the High Priestly Prayer Christ says: 'and now, Father, glorify thou me in thy own presence with the glory which I had with thee before the world was made' (John 17:5). 'Father, I desire that they also, whom thou hast given me, may be with me where I am, to behold my glory [the radiance of my being] which thou hast given me in thy love for me before the foundation of the world' (John 17:24). After all the developments from the time of Abraham the New Testament here finally arrives at clarity as to what THE SON is.

From this mystery of love in the Trinity the divine 'We' resounds in the Gospel of John. In the sentence 'I and the Father are One' (John 10:30), the word 'are'—*esmen*—indicates not the third but the first person plural, the 'We' being understood in the form of the verb. Therefore it reads: '(we) are one'. Similarly in the farewell speeches: 'If a man loves me, he will keep my word, and my Father will love him, and *we* will come to him and [*we* will] make *our* home with him' (John 14:23). In the Greek the italicized words do not occur, but the first person plural is indicated by the forms of the verbs, *eleusómetha*, *poiēsómetha*. In the High Priestly Prayer of Jesus this divine 'We' finally appears as a unique and special word: 'that they may be one, even as we are one' (John 17:11); 'that they also may be in us' (John 17:21), 'one even as we are one' (John 17:22). The great 'I am' of John's Gospel is raised in this 'We' to a new height.

It is a paradox that throughout the Koran Allah speaks of himself as 'We'. As a result he can only say 'I' in his absolute, transcendent isolation, and then only as the manifestation of an 'exclusive' I. If in the Koran the divine We is always used it is an appropriation of the royal plural, as it was used by kings. In the Koran this plural is merely a formality and has no other meaning or content. The *pluralis majestaticus* did once in former times have a meaning. In olden times a king was an initiate through whom higher beings were at work and he was not thought of as an individual person. In the Koran this royal We has no such actual spiritual background and taken literally it contradicts the exclusive uniqueness of Allah.

Humanity becoming Christian means that through the union of their being with THE SON men should come to share in this mystery. Only through fusion with him can they become 'sons of' their 'Father who is in heaven' (Matt.5:45). Luther shrank from the word 'sons' which nevertheless was the word given in the original text, and translated with the word 'children', and by so doing distorted the meaning of this passage. In Paul's letters we meet the word *hyothesia*—'being appointed to sonship'—again, not merely 'adoption', as Luther and the Authorized Version have it. 'For you did not receive the spirit of slavery to fall back into fear, but you have received the spirit of sonship' (Rom.8:15). This sonship has not yet been fully realized and we still 'groan inwardly' for it (Rom.8:23). In the Letter to the Galatians: 'God sent forth his Son . . . so that we might receive adoption as sons' (4:4–5). In the Letter to the Ephesians: 'He destined us in love to be his sons through Jesus Christ' (1:5). Through the eternal 'Son' God is for eternity 'Father'. Christ called him 'Father' in a still higher sense than men could. He distinguishes 'my Father and your Father' (John 20:17). But while they are growing into sonship men learn through the Spirit, as Paul said, to cry 'Abba!

Father!' (Rom.8:16). In the Lord's Prayer Christ gave his disciples the privilege of addressing God as 'Our Father'.

In contrast it can be important to observe that Allah is not addressed as father in Islam. The passages in the Koran where Allah's love is spoken of are completely isolated. 'O believers, whosoever of you turns from his religion, God will assuredly bring a people He loves and who love Him' (5:59). 'If you love God, follow me, and God will love you, and forgive you your sins; God is All-forgiving, All-compassionate, (3:29). A lot is said about the 'Compassionate', but Allah's compassion on closer examination proves to be the friendly whim of one who has absolute power, and who time and again displays no compassion at all. The way in which the Koran frequently repeats the sentence, 'God leads astray whomsoever he will' is nothing short of shocking. It is not merely a chance remark. 'What, do you desire to guide him whom God has led astray? Whom God leads astray, thou wilt not find for him a way' (4:90, see also 4:142; 6:125; 7:185; 13:27; 14:4; 16:39,95; 35:9; 42:41,45; 45:22; 74:34). The large number of passages cited shows this is not a case of a chance remark. 'Let the unbelievers not think that We prolong their days for their own good. We do so only that they may grow in wickedness. Theirs shall be a shameful punishment' (3:178 Dawood). Some have tried to soften Allah's 'leading astray' into permission for man to go his own way. According to Rudi Paret, however, the Arabic word in question can only be understood as 'to cause deliberately.'* The punishments of hell await those led astray by Allah. 'But My word shall be fulfilled: "I will fill the pit of Hell with jinn and men"' (32:13 Dawood). Although Allah leads astray, the erring are treated as responsible for their actions. 'He leads astray whom He will, and guides whom He will; and you will surely be questioned about the things you

---

* Rudi Paret, *Mohammed und der Koran*, p. 99.

wrought' (16:95). 'It is not for any soul to believe save by the leave of God; and He lays abomination upon those who have no understanding' (10:100). The denial of the 'Son' makes it difficult for Islam to conceive of independence and freedom alongside Allah's sole power. It was said of the enemy killed in the battle of Badr: 'You did not slay them, but God slew them' (8:17). 'Yet you cannot will, except by the will of Allah' (76:30 Dawood).

# Consequences in Mystical Thought

Allah, in contrast to all beings, exists in unbridgeable transcendence. Like all other creatures man exists only as a result of a mere word of command. We have already mentioned the saying, 'The likeness of Jesus, in God's sight, is as Adam's likeness; He created him of dust, then He said unto him, "Be," and he was' (3:52). This absolute command has no trace of the mystery of emanation, which in contrast a deeper understanding can find in the 'Word'. The speaking of the 'word' is 'utterance', 'communication with', indeed it has something of 'im-parting' about it. A speaker comes out of himself, he gives away something of himself, in the word as he expresses himself. By calling man into existence with his eternal name God shared with man some part of his own divinity. In this sense Paul in Athens made an expression from a hymn of Cleanthes (died 230 B.C.) his own: 'For we are indeed his offspring' (Acts 17:28). Allah's word of command, 'Be!' is in contrast a reduction to the superficially formal and is connected with a mood of 'only'. 'Allah forbid that He Himself should beget a son! When he decrees a thing He need only say: "Be," and it is' (19:36 Dawood. See also 36:82; 40:70). 'We have made all things according to a fixed decree. We command but once:

## Consequences in Mystical Thought

Our will is done in the twinkling of an eye' (54:49,50 Dawood). This image of 'the twinkling of an eye' gives characteristic expression to the lack of any creative sharing of self and the merely casual, almost magical action of supreme power. Men come into existence like all other 'things', and the concept of a son 'spoken' by the Father in eternity is completely excluded. For Christ's saying 'you are gods' (John 10:34), which points to the growth and development of the divine seed planted in men, there is no place in the Koran, just as there is no place for the saying in the First Letter of John about 'God's nature' in men (3:9). The external nature of the relationship between Allah and men effectively excludes any mystical thought, since mysticism seeks an inner experience of the divine. Later, however, an Islamic mysticism developed and spread from Persia, arising from the limited experience of converts to the Koran.

The Koran, however, with its doctrine of the absolute transcendence of God and its rejection of sonship exercised a powerful influence and caused the mysticism that arose within Islam to have a special character. Let a widely known mystical text of Jalâl al-Dîn known as Rumi (1207–73) be taken as an example. 'Someone knocked at the door of the loved one [God] and a voice within asked: "Who is there?" He answered: "It is I." And the voice said: "In this house there is no I and Thou." And the door stayed shut. Then the believer went into the wilderness and fasted and prayed. A year later he came again and knocked once more at the door. Again the voice asked: "Who is there?" and this time the believer answered: "It is Thou." Thereupon the door opened.' The religious longing for direct experience of God leads to man plunging as it were into the divine, completely abandoning his own individuality. Goethe, too, in the *West-Östlicher Divan* seized on the theme of the moth plunging into the flame for the deeply mystical poem '*Selige Sehnsucht*'. The goal for him, though, is not the total cessation of the individuality but only its purification in the fire of God; this destroys whatever cannot live together with God, so that a purified being arises from this death. 'Until you have it, this: Die and rise! you are nothing but a dismal guest on a dark earth.' He who is purified by the fire shall become a shining guest on this earth so needy of light. This is a Christian perception. In the text of Jalâl al-Dîn quoted above the significant sentence runs: 'In this house there is no I and Thou'. With Allah there is no room for another 'I', for a 'son'. While the Islamic believer stands too far from God as a 'slave', the Islamic mystic attempts excessive nearness, though with the loss of his individuality. At the second knocking at the door, by no longer saying, 'It is I' but 'It is Thou', he completely loses himself in the divine, and disappears into it.

Christian mysticism, particularly as it exists in the Gospel of John, is 'I-mysticism'. The Son's being one with the Father (John 10:30) develops into 'the Father is in me and I am in the Father' (10:38) and 'I am in the Father and the Father in me' (14:10). Whereas in the house of Allah there is no room for two 'I's, there the 'I's, both of the Son and of the Father, continue to exist. But each of the two 'I's can at any time absorb the other in itself. When we describe a man with a powerful ego as a 'closed personality' we mean that his ego holds the key to his own inner being. The ego refuses to let itself be inundated or alienated; it can lock itself against intruders. Mention is made in the Apocalypse of the one 'who has the key of David, who opens and no one shall shut, who shuts and no one opens' (Rev.3:7). The fact that man's ego can lock up the room of his personality, however, only presupposes the fact that he can also open it with complete sovereignty. We can really only invite another person to visit us in a room of which the key is in our control. The ability to lock up is there for the sake of the ability to unlock. In the same chapter of the Apocalypse there is a passage about Christ standing at the door and knocking. He respects man's control of the key and does not come like a housebreaker (John 10:10). 'If any one hears my voice and opens the door' (Rev.3:20)—this 'if any one' respects the freedom and free will of man. And when a man admits the Christ, the two do not merge in an undifferentiated unity, losing themselves in each other, but the two 'I's continue to exist in fellowship. 'I will come in to him and eat with him, and he with me' (Rev.3:20).

If we see in the ego only this 'closed state', then we can well come to think that this prison warder who locks us up in ourselves must be destroyed if we are to find 'the other'. But the greater the height to which the ego develops the more its ability to open and invite appears, by means of which it can receive 'the other' in its deepest recesses. The ego is an 'including' being which can absorb an infinite amount into itself.

The mysticism of Paul is in accord with this. 'It is no longer I who live, but Christ who lives in me' (Gal.2:20). This 'no longer I' in no way means the denial of the I-principle. This 'no longer I' is rather an actual achievement, which can come about only by means of an ego able to create space within itself and absorb what is to be let in; it does this by putting aside what it contains of its own selfish interests. Just as only I myself, and no one else, can say 'I' to me, so no other person either can say 'no longer I' on my behalf. If anyone else has to say this to me he must say 'no longer thou'. Only the 'I', within itself, has the power of stepping back and giving shelter to another. If the ego were destroyed, this shelter would also be lost. Paul's formula continues 'but Christ who lives in me'. 'In me'—that is to say in my ego, which therefore continues to exist after it has unselfishly achieved the withdrawal of itself into the 'no longer I'.

Love lives precisely in this: that two 'I's give each other

interior room and shelter. If someone who loves me were to cease being a 'Thou' for me, if he disappeared in me, how could I still love him? 'Love never ends' means too that the two distinct individualities continue to exist. And when these two love each other in self-forgetfulness, the forgotten self lives on in the consciousness of the other and is sheltered there.

The Islamic mystic Dahabe* explains the sentence 'I and thou no longer exist for us' by the words 'it would be untrue to speak of mine and thine'. Once more a contrasting passage is to be found in the Gospel of John. In the speech of farewell Christ said: 'All that the Father has is mine' (John 16:15), and in the High Priestly Prayer he continues: 'all mine are thine, and thine are mine' (John 17:10). Just as I and Thou live on as 'thou . . . in me, and I in thee' (John 17:21), the mine and thine do not lose their meaning in this fellowship of love, nor do they become untrue. While what is mine is always being experienced afresh as what is thine, and what is thine as what is mine, 'love never ends'.

In Christian thought, the divine 'I' is not exclusive like Allah, but inclusive. It is an *'ens communicativum sui'*, as the schoolman said: a being whose characteristic it is to share itself and by the gift of part of itself to make it possible for other beings to participate in the divine. Monotheism is not harmed by this if we cite the already mentioned words of John about God's seed within man, or the passage in the Second Letter of Peter about the divine nature (*theia physis*) of which we may become partakers (1:4).

In contrast to this, when the mystic, Hallāj, who was executed as a heretic under the Muslim orthodoxy in 922, said about himself, 'I am God', it had quite a different nuance. He meant that his being God was not thanks to a share in the divine

---

* Quoted from Carl Clemen, *Die Nichtchristlichen Kulturreligionen*, Part II, p. 77.

having been granted him but because of an identification with God which obliterates every trace of his separate individuality.

It is in its own way logical, too, that Islamic mysticism should time and again lead to the dervish cults. As a blow against rational comprehension, Jalâl al-Dîn founded a dervish order. The numerous dervish orders all strive for ecstacy by various methods, amongst which a part is played by the ceaseless rhythmical chanting of the formula 'la ilaha ill'Allah' (there is no God but Allah). It is reported that Jalâl al-Dîn used to dance a particular kind of whirling dance for hours on end.* The 'dancing' and the 'howling' dervishes work themselves up into a state of trance, in which it is possible for the body to be insensitive to injury or for wounds to heal with astonishing speed. This depends on extinguishing the ego of daily consciousness and producing an ego-less condition. In the Acts of the Apostles there is an account of how Paul described his Damascus experience to the procurator Festus and King Agrippa. Festus surmised that Paul had had an ecstatic experience, a divine 'frenzy', that is to say, being in an ego-less condition such as the dervishes later strove to attain. 'Paul, you are mad'. The answer came: 'I am not mad ... but I am speaking the sober truth' (Acts 26:24,25). For 'sober' the word in the Greek text is sōphrosýne. We meet this word as a verb in the Gospel account of the man possessed in Gerasa. He had raved in frenzy and the people find him later sitting by Jesus 'clothed and in his right mind (sophronounta)', brought back into the clear ego-centred everyday consciousness (Mark 5:15; Luke 8:35).

Again and again in the Koran we meet the sentence 'to Allah is the homecoming'. It is possible to perceive in this the basic tone of religious life, but we must also ask how this returning home to Allah is conceived. The Godhead has allowed man to

* Emil Dermengham, Mohammed, p. 152.

develop in a cosmic evolution until at last he reached the point where he was inwardly aware of himself as an independent being. At first the self-realization of the individual was darkened by egotistical characteristics and was accompanied by the consequent detachment from the heavenly homeland; this resulted in the isolation of earthly man in ego-solitude. Man has to find his way to the divine home again. He can look for this way by going backwards and returning to the point whence he set out. This involves shedding everything that has developed as personal life; thus the egotistical characteristics go, but the self-awareness that has been won is lost too. The entire earthly path with all its suffering appears to be the 'wrong' way and is rejected. Man then flows back again into the ocean of the divine and loses himself completely in it. Everything is again as it once was before the beginning, just as if nothing had happened in between. This kind of 'coming home', involving the loss of the ego developed on earth, is also an active part of Buddhist striving for nirvana. The attitude in Richard Wagner's *Tristan and Isolde* provides an example of this when the *Liebestod* (love-death) is glorified as 'drowning—submerging —unconscious—highest joy'. Reminiscent of the Buddhist ideal of nirvana was the similar concept of *fana* introduced by the Persian Muslim mystic, Bistāmī, also called Bāyazid (died *c.* 875) as a way of self-annihilation in divine frenzy,[*] although the Koran, with its doctrine of an external creation, in fact allows absolutely no possibility whatever of flowing back into the primal divine substance. In the *fana*, the ego-consciousness flows back entirely into God's consciousness and becomes indiscriminately identical with it; consequently Bistāmī can say: 'Truly I am God, there is no other God but me, worship me. How great indeed is my Majesty'. The peaceful nirvana here takes on the character of a desperately bold leap into the

[*] Tiele-Söderblom, *Kompendium der Religionsgeschichte*, p. 169.

purely divine, brushing everything else aside. With a 'coming home' to God of this nature the great organization of creative forces which in the course of aeons has finally led to the emergence of a free mankind on earth would have to be declared worthless. Everything would be again as it was in the beginning and the entire divine effort would be wasted.

The other possible way home to God lies in striving forwards. The independence achieved by emancipated earthly man would then have to be freed from the egoism that has crept in and overshadowed it; independence would then be developed into the selflessness of the ego. Having become independent, man is to return from his isolation as 'son'. Earthly man is not able to do this with his own resources. But the Christ in his mercy has come down to him in order to lift him up into sonship and so bring him home together with what he has attained on earth. Man imbued with Christ can then bring with him something from the earth which could not have come into existence in just that way in heaven alone. Should not the gift of individuality allotted to man be considered the subject of the Gospel parable of the talents, in which the master reproaches the slothful servant, saying that he should have worked with what had been entrusted to him? The slothful servant returns the 'talent' he had been given exactly as he received it. His master, however, expected the amount to have been increased, 'and at my coming I should have received what was my own with interest' (Matt.25:27). The master wants to receive 'my own' (*to emón*)—the ego-substance placed at the servant's disposal—with interest, with growth. The entire development of man on earth can result in an enrichment of the realm of heaven, thanks to the sacrifice of Christ.

# Moon Year versus Sun Year

A certain relationship to the moon is common to both the Old Testament and Islam. By the moon we do not mean the dead matter in space but a particular quality, a particular supersensible essence.* It is known that the moon played a large part in the ancient cult of Yahweh. Just as the monotheism of the Old Testament left the way open for the acceptance of trinitarian doctrines, the moon-like features of the Old Testament leave the way open for the acceptance of sun-like features, which are in particular connected with the Christ, with the 'Son'. The sun-like quality of the Christ is clearly perceptible in the New Testament. After Peter had uttered his avowal that Jesus was the Son of God, the three disciples on the mountain of the transfiguration saw the face of Jesus 'like the sun' (Matt.17:2). Paul saw the Risen Lord on the road to Damascus in a light 'brighter than the sun' (Acts 26:13). On Patmos, John saw the face of the Son of Man shining 'like the sun . . . in full strength' (Rev.1:16). The death on Golgotha made the sun lose its light. The Resurrection took place on the day of the sun, and in the ever continuing octaves of that day Christianity celebrates its Sunday. It was on a Sunday that John received the Apocalypse. The Christ-event is the pulse that goes on beating in the rhythm of the Christian year. The Christian year is a sun year, with Christmas at the winter solstice and Easter at the constellation of sun and moon after the spring equinox. The religious rites of Christianity are closely bound up with the year.

Muhammad put an axe to the root of this idea of experiencing the sun's year in close connection with the divine Son. On his farewell pilgrimage to Mecca—even after the conquest of Mecca he continued to live at Medina—in the spring of 632,

* On the 'sun-like' and 'moon-like' in the Bible, see Emil Bock, *Urgeschichte*.

## Moon Year versus Sun Year

Muhammad proclaimed with the highest authority that the moon's year must be completely and absolutely adhered to. 'The number of months, with God, is twelve in the Book of God, the day that He created the heavens and the earth' (9:36). 'The month postponed is an increase of unbelief whereby the unbelievers go astray. One year they make it profane [postponing it by intercalary days or months] and hallow it another, to agree with the number that God has hallowed, and so profane what God has hallowed' (9:37). If one goes exactly by the twelve moons of the year one gets a year of 354 days, eleven days too few for the sun's year. In order to keep in step with the sun's year, with the actual solstices and equinoxes, it is necessary to make additions to the pure moon year. By so doing it is possible to keep in step with the sun, but it is not possible to keep the months exactly in step with the phases of the moon. In former times the sun's year, which is indeed nature's year, had been adhered to in Arabia by means of intercalation. Muhammad now changed all this.

The Islamic year has in consequence only 354 days and begins each new year eleven days early. This error accumulates from one year to another and as a result the year's feast days get misplaced. The month of fasting, Ramadan, sets out on its travels, and thirty-three years go by before, having travelled through the entire cycle of the year, it turns up again at the point from which it set out. After thirty-three years the annual mistakes have accumulated sufficiently for it once again to be 'in order'. In thirty-three sun years there are therefore thirty-four moon years. The span of the year is not only separated from any base in nature but chronology itself is confused. Christian chronology with its 'before' and 'after Christ' contrasts with Islamic chronology which views the hegira, Muhammad's migration from Mecca to Medina, as the starting point of the new era. This migration took place in the autumn of 622. The New Year's Day which in 622 fell on July 15/16 is taken as the first day of the new era. In each century the Islamic chronology gains three additional moon years. This explains why in 1977 Islam has not attained A.H. (*anno Hegirae*) 1355 (1977 minus 622) but has already moved on to A.H. 1397.

The introduction of the strict lunar year sought to discredit our Christian year completely as 'the year of the Lord'. The imposition of this lunar year strikingly symbolizes the reality that the moon and the moon-like in Islam are rigidly closed to the sun and the sun-like. As a result Islam can seem to be a revived Old Testament doctrine which to some extent has been 'sterilized' by being robbed of its sun potential.

Together with the denial of the 'Son', this attack on the sun year reveals a very serious difference between Christianity and Islam which cannot easily be ignored.

# An Approach to Recognition of the Son

The nature of man is prepared for the mystery of the Son. The purpose of all human development is expressed at the end of the Apocalypse, where God says of the man 'who conquers': 'I will be his God and he shall be my son' (Rev.21:7). The Muslim conception of man as Allah's slave lacks this purpose, because it rejects the mystery of the Son. Nevertheless, the Koran contains an important approach to a more profound perception of the nature of man.

The Koran mentions several times a Jewish legend which deals with the special vocation of man. This story is found in the Second Sura:

And when thy Lord [Allah is speaking to Muhammad] said to the angels, 'I am setting in the earth a viceroy.' They said, 'What, wilt Thou set therein one who will do corruption there, and shed blood, while We proclaim Thy praise and call Thee Holy?' He said, 'Assuredly I know that you know not.' And He taught Adam the names, all of them; then He presented them unto the angels and said, 'Now tell Me the names of these, if you speak truly.' They said, 'Glory be to Thee! We know not save what Thou has taught us. Surely Thou art the All-knowing, the All-wise.' He said, 'Adam, tell them their names.' And when he had told them their names He said, 'Did I not tell you I know the unseen things of the heavens and earth? And I know what things you reveal, and what you were hiding.' And when We said to the angels, 'Bow yourselves to Adam'; so they bowed themselves, save Iblis [*Diabolos, Lucifer*]; he refused, and waxed proud . . . (2:28–32, and also 7:10–12; 15:26–43; 17:63–66; 18:48; 20:115).

This Jewish legend is connected with the second chapter of Genesis: 'So out of the ground the LORD God formed every beast of the field and every bird of the air, and brought them to the man [Adam] to see what he would call them; and whatever the man called every living creature, that was its name' (Gen.2:19,20). The legend takes the matter further. It says that the angels expressed their disapproval of the creation of man, when the Lord questioned them about it. Thereupon the Lord brought every kind of animal before the angels and asked the angels the names of the animals. They could not answer. Immediately God asked Adam the same question and he could say their names, and furthermore when God asked him he was able to state his own name and even the Lord's name of Yahweh. The worship of man by the angels is found in the Talmud.

Lucifer, 'Iblis' in the Koran, refused to prostrate himself before Adam. 'So they bowed themselves, save Iblis—he was not of those that bowed themselves. Said He, "What prevented thee to bow thyself, when I commanded thee?" Said he: "I am better than he; Thou createdst me of fire, and him Thou createdst of clay" ' (7:10,11). Sura 15 is even clearer: 'And when thy Lord said to the angels, "See, I am creating a mortal of a clay and mud moulded. When I have shaped him, and breathed My spirit in him, fall you down, bowing before him!" Then all the angels bowed themselves all together, save Iblis; he refused to be among those bowing. Said He, "What ails thee, Iblis, that thou art not among those bowing?" Said he, "I would never bow myself before a mortal whom Thou has created of a clay of mud moulded" ' (15:28–33).

The angels, the nine grades of whose hierarchy up to cherubim and seraphim have been described by Dionysius the Areopagite, are something like 'older brothers' of man in the development of the worlds. In the twentieth century Rudolf Steiner in the course of a modern spiritual research has confirmed the old knowledge of the nine grades of angels and has given a detailed description of their part in the coming into being of the worlds.* In the highest place are the seraphim, close beside God. The lowest level, immediately above man, is occupied by the angels, the *angeloi*. The name 'angel' can also be used in a general sense for all the nine ranks. The higher the rank of these supersensible spiritual beings, the nearer to God is their consciousness and the more powerful is their influence. They accomplished their development in long past states of the universe, when the evolving earth had not yet achieved its present dense material structure but still retained a finer, more ethereal kind of existence. The spiritual realm of men would be a tenth rank in the hierarchy, beneath the angels. But the hierarchical rank of human spirits experienced the decisive stage of its coming into existence in a period of the universe in which the earth underwent the process of thickening and

* Rudolf Steiner, *Occult Science—an Outline*.

condensing into coarse material. As the human spirit took bodily form on the earth it had to accept a body condensed to the hardness of bone, which brought death with it as an inescapable destiny. The legend reflects images of this difference: the angels 'live above in light', above death. They look down with resentment on this tenth rank in the hierarchy which is to grow and follow them there. They themselves do not know what it is to be embodied in this way 'in the flesh', and therefore do not know death. The angels foresee that man, embodied in flesh and living as if in an isolation cell in his physical body, will be able to emancipate himself from the upper world and thereby bring destruction and bloodshed to the earth. They do not rightly understand, as it were, how God can take such a risk, and what he can find that is so great about this endangered and dangerous realm of men. The legend makes Lucifer, the proud angel, refer to the finer element of his existence: 'Thou createdst me of fire, and him Thou createdst of clay.' This need not imply that man is merely 'earth', but it is an expression of the fact that man in his soul and spirit has undergone a connection with earthly materiality which weighs heavily on him and which is of the deepest significance for his entire consciousness. Abraham felt deeply this element in his being when he stood before God—'I who am but dust and ashes' (Gen.18:27). The legend says, however, that the Lord God, knowing full well the risk and hazard connected with 'Operation Man' perceived something of great value beyond all the negative features. 'I know that you know not'. He knows that man's freedom from the primal divine no longer allows him to be so obviously an 'angel' as the nine grades above him; on the other hand he knows that this freedom offers the opportunity for a free spiritual being to develop, which at first will become 'freed from God' in a tragic way, in order to be able to become 'free for God' in the fullest sense, precisely because of this estrangement—but with the help of grace through the Christ. The higher ranks of the hierarchy living 'in light' are, as it were, in accordance with their spiritual nature, still so close to the divine that they are absolutely incapable of reaching such a level of independence as earthly man. Earthly man can indeed in his detachment become an atheist, which an angel could never do. The reverse side of the possibility of atheism is a freedom of will which is completely without mental inhibitions and which arises without any coercion. This is the freedom, as an independent ego being, to conclude the 'New Covenant' with the great ego of God, which appears on earth in Christ as THE SON and offers itself freely to man. With this lofty and distant goal before his eyes the Lord can accept the angels' misgivings about the danger of the experiment with man.

He gives the angels an impression of the specific value, of the 'plus' beyond the capacity of angels, which man is going to produce, although his position is beneath the angels. He gives them this impression by allowing the man to name the creatures. The names are the ideas, God's thoughts of these beings. In the Koran the giving of names extends to all things. Man can from his own emancipated consciousness discover and pronounce the thoughts of God, which are the foundations of the created world. By recognizing the contents of the world in his own self he creates them all afresh, as it were, and is able to reflect the Creator's work back to him.

In both the Jewish and the Koran versions of this legend the angels are made to prostrate themselves and worship Adam. This is quite astonishing from the point of view of both Old Testament and Islamic piety. It can really only be justified by looking prophetically forward to the future fulfilment, which again is dependent on the Logos becoming flesh in a human body. In one passage in the New Testament there is a suggestion that Christ's achievement on earth is an event which can make

the angels look longingly down from the realms of light, full
of spiritual desire. What happened at Golgotha did not happen
in heaven, but on earth, in man's realm. The Gospel preached
'things into which angels long to look' (1Pet.1:12).

It is precisely the fact that man lives beneath the hierarchy of
angels in an earthly body that creates the opportunity for the
divine Son to lift him up from above over all nine ranks of
angels into 'sonship'. As Muhammad did not know the mystery
of the Son, the legend he adapted remains an approach which
never attained complete development. All the same it is
important that man appears for once as God's viceroy on
earth, and not as his slave. In the original Arab text the word
*khalīfa* occurs in this passage, that is to say 'caliph' (2:28).

One other passage in the Koran should be mentioned in this
connection. It occurs rather erratically as a section at the end
of Sura 33. 'We offered Our trust to the heavens, to the earth,
and to the mountains, but they refused the burden and were
afraid to receive it. Man undertook to bear it, but he has proved
a sinner and a fool' (33:72 Dawood). Here, at the beginning of
the development of the world, man is regarded as a pre-existing
spiritual being, as an 'Adam Cadmon', as the original spiritual
Man. He has a singular relationship with God. It is a question
of what Henning's German translation calls '*das Unterpfand*',
the pledge or the pawn. In Arabic the word is '*amāna*'. The
Ahmadija translation reads '*Vertrauenspfand*', pledge of trust.
In English translations 'truth' and 'faith' are found, as well as
trust. Henri Corbin in his *Histoire de la philosophie islamique*
renders it as '*le dépôt de nos secrets*'. '*Amāna*' is from the same
root as 'amen' as 'believe' in the story of Abraham when God
led Abraham outside and he looked towards heaven with its
stars and 'believed'. Somehow or other it is a matter of a
covenant of trust which God concluded with the man. God
first of all offered the '*amāna*' to the spiritual powers, to the

hierarchical beings who in olden times could still be seen by clairvoyance to be at work in the cosmic phenomena—in the skies, on the earth, in the mountains. But these beings refused. They did not want to go beyond what they carried out as their God-given duties in the framework of creation. So God then passed by the hierarchies and came to man and offered him this special relationship. This has always been represented as God asking man if he were willing to enter into a special relationship based on obedience, making God's law his own, with the prospect of reward in Paradise, but also the risk of damnation in hell if he should fail to fulfil the contract. On the one hand a splendid goal, on the other hand a dangerous abyss. And lo and behold, Adam said 'Yes'. He agreed to the proposal carelessly, as it appears, and without reflection—'he has proved a sinner and a fool'. Later Islamic thinkers, however, were willing to see in this negative estimation of man something that was not merely derogatory. They understood it as a recognition that man had the courage to take a risk, advancing boldly on a dangerous undertaking, in something like the spirit of a Faust.

This verse of the Koran, which sounds to us like a grandiose fragment of mythology, contains an understanding of the special position of man and the divine daring of 'Operation Man', a daring which is ready to accept the possibility of a double outcome, because what is involved is freedom. This special relationship between the God daring to take the risk and the man prepared to accept it rests on *amāna*, on the 'amen' power of the completest trust, of a belief—not merely of man in God, but originally of a belief of God in man.

Once more this superb intuition remains isolated in the Koran. Here, too, his denial of the 'Son' prevents Muhammad from developing further this highly important and vital approach towards a penetrating understanding of man. He encountered Christianity in such an undeveloped form, and was so far from a proper understanding of its own mysteries, that he was unable to perceive its essence. The words of one of the Mecca Suras strike us as tragic: 'If the Lord of Mercy had a son, I would be the first to worship him' (43:81 Dawood).

# IV

# Islam and Arab Culture

## Arabian Scientific Achievement

Before Muhammad's time world history had on the whole passed Arabia by. Neither Alexander the Great nor the Roman Empire, neither Persia nor Byzantium had been able to conquer this peninsula, so well protected by large expanses of desert. What happened after Muhammad's appearance is all the more surprising. The people of Arabia, after they had been united by the Prophet, broke out of their frontiers with nothing short of explosive force. They were impelled by the power of the religion of Islam. The force of this expansion was fantastic. Some well known facts can be run over once more. Muhammad died in Medina in 632. Just six years after his death the caliph Umar entered Jerusalem on a white camel. By 650 Syria, Palestine and Egypt had been torn from the Byzantine Empire, and the Persian kingdom conquered. At the end of the century the Arabs had subdued all North Africa, which ceased to be a Christian country. In 711 they crossed over into Spain. They overthrew the West Gothic kingdom and pressed on through all Spain right up to the Pyrenees. A hundred years after Muhammad's death they were advancing deep into France. At Tours and Poitiers, Christian Western Europe had difficulty in resisting this previously unknown desert people, who had broken out of the Arabian peninsula. In the east they advanced as far as the Indus. Byzantium had with difficulty held them for the time being. This trail of conquest was a military miracle, which was quickly followed by a second miracle. The bedouin armies were still very primitive at the outset, but after they had settled on the cultivated ground of a higher culture they undertook the spiritual conquest of the civilized values of each land and on this foundation built up their own characteristic culture. In 687 an Umayyad Prince in Damascus initiated the translation into Arabic of Greek scientific works. The caliphate was then transferred from the Umayyads in Damascus to the Abbāsids in Baghdad. They were descendants of Abbās, an uncle of Muhammad. Under the caliphs Harun al Rashid (786–809) and Mamūn (813–833) the development of this culture proceeded with great brilliance.

Grasping eagerly at the intellectual wealth of Greek culture, the Arabs attached themselves to the work already in progress of translating Greek books into Syrian. This had already been going on for some time when Islam first came into existence. These Syrian translations from the Greek were in fact the work of Nestorian Christian scholars who could not work in the Byzantine Empire because of their adherence to the Nestorian heresy. They could, however, work in the new Persian state of the Sassanids. Henri Corbin wrote about this situation: 'Bearing in mind these Greek–Syrian translations, the great translation enterprise which took shape three centuries after the hegira seems more like a methodical and comprehensive continuation of work already successfully accomplished than a new undertaking.'* Some of the Greek texts were translated direct into Arabic, some were translated from the Syrian versions.

The western equivalent to Baghdad was the marvellous refinement of Moorish culture which arose under a branch of the Umayyads in Cordoba from the middle of the eighth century. The civilization which then came into being in Baghdad and Cordoba was incomparably superior to the

* Henri Corbin, *Histoire de la philosophie islamique*, p. 33.

contemporary civilization of Christian Europe.* Another seven centuries had to pass before Europe from its own resources could equal the Arab achievement.

This remarkable success resulted from a particular outlook. It was characteristic of the Arab genius to be interested in a rather one-sided way in the material aspects of our world. It was especially gifted in the natural sciences, in particular where they can be mastered by the calculating intellect. Their interest embraced above all that part of the discoveries in the classical cultural heritage which embraced mathematics, astronomy, geography, medicine, chemistry, botany and zoology. All these were absorbed with a great thirst for knowledge and were also further developed and added to with self-confidence.

The young nations of Christian Europe had completely neglected precisely this part of the classical heritage which had been cultivated at Alexandria. Because of the character of medieval Christianity, souls were directed with a certain one-sidedness towards the hereafter. Christian spiritual leaders of that time did not feel at all uneasy because they did not know how, for instance, optical laws functioned. Arabian scholars were troubled deeply by precisely such questions. They developed methods of research free from presupposition, using objective observation and patient experimentation. Their attitude of mind was already the attitude which is generally accepted today as that of a natural scientist.

These achievements of Arab culture, magnificent in their field, are, to use Biblical language, the fulfilment of the blessing which promised Ishmael a great future. Divine Providence looks a long way ahead. The Bible describes how Providence on the one hand had the legitimate line in mind which was to lead from Abraham through Isaac to an event bringing universal salvation; on the other hand it describes how care

* Compare Sigrid Hunke, *Allahs Sonne über dem Abendland*.

was taken to prevent the 'Ishmael' branch from disappearing. 'Ishmael' was singled out, as it were, for a task which at that time lay in the distant future. Only in the seventh century after Christ was it first realized. By then Christianity had already come into existence, but it was still a long way from real maturity, far from imbuing humanity with the Christ. This requires a number of stages of development. The young Christian nations of Europe had indeed taken Christianity deep into their hearts, but because of their kind of piety they were so one-sidedly concentrated on the hereafter that frequently the things of this world were only experienced in a dream-like state of consciousness. A piety such as this which loses the earth under its feet cannot in the last analysis really come up to the requirements of Christianity. It is precisely in intercourse with the realities of *this* world that a certain inner awareness in selfless attentiveness can be trained which will then one day help the change of direction to 'above'. A level of awareness can be gained in things of this world which is capable of developing into higher spiritual perception.

Rudolf Steiner has shown in his study of Christianity that, with the passage of time, tributaries developing independently outside Christianity have time and again flowed into Christianity and enriched its course. Rudolf Steiner said, 'the greatest impulse given to the human intellect was brought by the Arabians. Without thorough knowledge of the course taken by the evolution of humanity it is impossible to form any idea of how much the world-conception which arose in a new form under the symbol of the Moon, has given to mankind. There could have been no Kepler, no Galileo, without the impulses which were brought by Arabism into Europe.'*

This 'greatest stimulus for the human intellect', originating

* Rudolf Steiner, *Background to the Gospel of St. Mark*, Lecture 9, p. 150.

101

outside the Christian world, must at first have affected Christendom merely as a terrible and devastating blow from an unexpected quarter. In the long term it had the task of leading European Christianity to complete earthly awareness of this world; only when this clear consciousness is its starting point can Christianity move towards clearer spiritual perception of the supersensible, and above all of the true meaning of the Mystery of Golgotha. If Christianity is to carry enlightenment for future times and be inspired by the Holy Spirit, intellectual activity must be really absorbed in genuine expansion of consciousness, and human intelligence transformed into higher spiritual vision.

Without this challenging intellectual activity there will not be the necessary advance in consciousness to a Christianity that is aware of the depths of its own mysteries. Only if Christianity can struggle to achieve such an illumination of consciousness can 'Ishmael' fulfil his mission. And only then will Arab culture's harsh and unexpected blow finally take a positive place in a sufficiently broad Christian view of history. If Christianity cannot meet this challenge of consciousness, then humanity will more and more lose its way in the blind alley of materialism. The scientific movement of the Arabs began with the enthusiasm of discoverers for what could be observed and calculated. But this is only a part of total reality. If knowledge stops in this limited territory, the longer such one-sidedness continues the more disastrous will be its effect. Despite all its intellectual brilliance and technical perfection it must lead to increasing cultural decline, and eventually, when it has consumed all the spiritual heritage it has taken from the past, to cultural death.

The Arab culture we have in mind as 'the greatest impulse given to the human intellect' is not simply to be equated with Islam, which of course in another sense is a part of Arab culture.

Islam as a religion precedes the Arab culture which stimulated a scientific civilization. The Arabs would have stayed in their isolated peninsula had it not been for the driving force of a fanatical belief. The astonishing thing is the speed with which the conquering bands, borne on the wings of religious fanaticism, shed their bedouin character and transformed themselves into upholders of civilization. The world of the refined Arab scholars is a different world from the world of the Koran. On one side were the accurate achievements of the highest order in the natural sciences which have already been mentioned—for example, experiments in optics, calculation of the circumference of the earth, the theory of equations. On the other side were the primitive statements in the Koran, such as the injunction to lock up and beat disobedient women (4:38), and the injunction to cut off the hands of thieves (5:42). Science as developed by the Arabs, and the Koran are in a sense outwardly opposed to each other, although again they are not entirely unconnected. Islam was the vehicle which carried Arab men out into the wide world. Islam also contains elements by means of which it provides a preparation for the Arab attitude of mind and points the way to it.

# Islam as the Forerunner of Arabism

The old pagan world with its many gods points to the earlier instinctive clairvoyance, which still perceived some of the manifold spiritual beings which are actually behind the phenomena of the world and active in them. This clairvoyance was lost. The gods became idols, religious worship became entangled in superficialities, and confused the sensible and the supersensible planes in a superstitious way. The monotheism of the Old Testament and of Islam focuses its gaze on the highest unity. The increasing awareness in man of his own individuality enabled him to grasp the idea of a corresponding divine individuality, though at first rather abstractly. Religious feeling was concentrated on the high peak of this unity; the phenomena of the world, devoid of divinities because of the decline of paganism, thus became profane. They became mere created objects, which could be approached without inhibition by the intellect in its hunger for knowledge. This opened the way for an entirely intellectual approach to the phenomena of the world by means of calculation. The genius of Arab culture was specially well equipped for such an outlook.

Natural science in this sense is not included in the Koran, but there are some things that prepare the way for it. Tradition has preserved a saying of Muhammad, which is not in the Koran, that knowledge should be sought throughout life: 'He who strives after knowledge prays to God'.* This does not mean a knowledge that initiates into a higher realm or a knowledge that searches 'the depths of God' (1Cor.2:10) with spiritual inspiration; it means the knowledge of this world which the intellect can acquire and which at that time the genius of Arab culture set about acquiring, seeing this as its own particular task. This type of knowledge is viewed with a kind of naïve respect in the Koran.

Mathematics, calculation, is essential in a search for knowledge of this kind. In this connection it is characteristic that a special quality of Allah is continually praised. 'God is swift at the reckoning' is said with reference to calculation of merit or guilt on the Day of Judgment. This is not a casual expression, but one that occurs so often in the Koran that it is absolutely impossible to overlook it; it must be evaluated as a characteristic feature of the conception of God in the Koran

* Sigrid Hunke, *Allahs Sonne über dem Abendland*, p. 203.

(2:198; 3:17,199; 5:6; 6:62; 21:48; 40:17; 72:28). Also in this category belongs the statement that 'Allah is the supreme Plotter' (3:55 Dawood) who contrived a plan for Jesus whereby he was able to snatch him away from death at the hands of the Jews.

Muhammad forbade the drinking of wine as a practice which threatens clear, sober consciousness. 'They ask you about drinking and gambling. Say: "There is great harm in both, although they have some benefit for men; but their harm is far greater than their benefit" ' (2:219 Dawood). 'Believers, wine and games of chance, idols and divining arrows, are abominations devised by Satan. Avoid them, so that you may prosper. Satan seeks to stir up enmity and hatred among you by means of wine and gambling, and to keep you from the remembrance of Allah and from your prayers. Will you not abstain from them? Obey Allah, and obey the Apostle. Beware' (5:91,92 Dawood).

The Koran repeatedly appeals to rational thought. 'Surely in the creation of the heavens and earth and in the alternation of night and day there are signs for men possessed of minds' (3:187; also 24:44). 'It is He that has created for you the stars, so that they may guide you in the darkness of land and sea. We have made plain Our revelations to men of wisdom.' 'It was He that created you from *one* being . . . We have made plain Our revelations to men of understanding' (6:97–98 Dawood). These signs are valid not only for 'true believers' (6:99 Dawood) but just as much for other people who think. 'Thus we make plain Our revelations to men of understanding' (7:33 Dawood). 'The likeness of this present life is as water that We send down out of heaven . . . Even so We distinguish the signs for a people who reflect' (10:25). 'And perform the prayer at the two ends of the day and nigh of the night; surely the good deeds will drive away the evil deeds. That is a remembrance unto the mindful' (11:116). 'And He subjected to you the night and the day, and the sun and the moon; and the stars are subjected by His command. Surely in that are signs for a people who understand' (16:12). At the end of the sura which contains the story of Joseph, this passage occurs: 'In their [the prophets'] stories is surely a lesson to men possessed of minds' (12:111). 'And of His signs is your slumbering by night . . . Surely in that are signs for a people who hear' (30:22). In lightning and in rain too there are 'signs for a people who understand' (30:23). 'So We distinguish the signs for a people who understand' (30:27). 'And in the turning about of the winds there are signs for a people who understand' (45:4). 'If we had sent down this Koran upon a mountain, thou wouldst have seen it humbled, split asunder out of the fear of God. And those similitudes—We strike them for men; haply they will reflect' (59:21). Even the battle of Badr, where a small force defeated a larger one, 'is a lesson for men possessed of eyes' (3:11).

Islam also appealed to the rational mind in being so clear and lucid. It could be rationally summarized in a few sentences. The concept of one God was much more readily comprehensible by abstract thought than the mystery of a God who was both One and Three. The merely human relationship of the Prophet to Allah likewise presented no difficulties to the mind, as opposed to the mysteries of the Incarnation of God, which nevertheless are not beneath the level of rational understanding, but above it, revealing themselves only to a higher perception developed through the Holy Spirit. Christian theology, which no longer had any esoteric knowledge, declared too early that it was content to be able to show, if necessary, that the Christian mysteries were not entirely inconsistent with rational thinking, but that they were virtually barred to rational comprehension and had to be believed in on authority. Only an enlightened Christianity, and not one that abandons reason, can be a match for Islam's indestructible delight in knowledge, even if this knowledge is confined to rationalism.

# The Book

The fact that Islam, to a greater extent than any other religion, attributes decisive importance to the book, indeed to the book 'as such', also helped to develop the Arab scientific impulse.

Muhammad's encounter with Judaism played an important part here. Judaism had become in the highest degree a book religion. Jewry impressed Muhammad as a 'people of the book' and this impression was extended to include the Christians as well. The development of late Judaism into a book religion can clearly be seen in the Old Testament. In the time of the Maccabees, that is to say in the second century B.C., people realized that the prophetic voice with which Yahweh had spoken directly—'Thus says the LORD'—was silent (1 Macc. 4:46; 9:27; 14:41), and had been so since the fifth century. In the period after the return from Babylon and the reconstruction of the Temple, Judaism had two outstanding religious leaders, Ezra and Nehemia. They no longer worked as the prophets had done. They carefully collected the sacred writings and so laid the foundations for the Bible. Looking back on that time the Second Book of the Maccabees says: '[Nehemia] founded a library [*bibliothéke*] and collected the books about the kings and prophets, and the writings of David . . . In the same way Judas also collected all the books that had been lost' (2 Macc. 2:13–14). Ezra was the first of the 'book scholars'. Ezra 'was a scribe skilled in the law of Moses' (Ezra 7:6). The Hebrew word for scribe is *sofer*—the man of books. The powerful impression made by Ezra is reflected in the criticism of the Jews which the

Koran unjustly made 'The Jews say, "Ezra is the Son of God"'
(9:30). By the time of the Maccabees scribes are already very
numerous, and they play an important part (1Macc.7:12). After
the destruction of Jerusalem by the Romans the Synod of
Jamnia determined the Canon of the Jewish Bible, whose words
had divine authority. This was in the last decade of the first
Christian century.

The word 'book' appears for the first time in the Old
Testament in the 5th chapter of Genesis. 'This is the book of
the generations of Adam' (5:1). By 'book' the genealogical
register is meant, the enumeration of names from Adam up to
Noah and his sons, which are booked or entered in this register.
Clearly referring to this, Matthew begins his New Testament
Gospel with the words, 'The book of the genealogy of Jesus
Christ' (Matt.1:1), in this way stressing that the names from
Abraham to Jesus are 'booked' or entered in the register. The
'book' later in the Old Testament appears as a visionary record,
as an image through which supersensible reality can be
glimpsed. In his apocalyptic dream Daniel saw the Day of
Judgment. 'The court sat in judgment, and the books were
opened' (Dan.7:10). The same image is given to John. The
dead are standing before the throne of God 'and books were
opened' (Rev.20:12). 'Books', in the plural, on the basis of
which the dead are judged. Every person has his 'book'. In his
earthly existence he made entries in a supersensible substance
in the universe in which his good and evil deeds are booked or
entered as though in the memory of the universe. He will
eventually be confronted with this record. John's vision goes
further than Daniel's, adding a 'book of life' to the individual biographies, a register of all humanity. The point is
that a man is represented by entries even in the higher realm
of divine life. If he has entries in this realm, his name is
written 'in the book of life' (Rev.20:12,15; 21:27; 3:5). The

# The Book

Apocalypse also uses the image of the 'book' in various other ways (5:1; 10:2).

Similarly the Koran, in harmony with the biblical vision of the world, knows the book as a record. 'Didst thou not know that God knows all that is in heaven and earth? Surely that is in a Book' (22:69). 'Every term has a Book' (13:38). So does every individual. Here the image is the same as in Daniel and John. At the Last Judgment each individual book of fate will be opened. 'And every man—We have fastened to him his bird of omen upon his neck; and We shall bring forth for him, on the Day of Resurrection, a book he shall find spread wide open. "Read thy book! Thy soul suffices thee this day as a reckoner against thee" ' (17:14–15). Here there is also the idea of a man having himself to pronounce the verdict. The just man will be given his book in his right hand, the unjust man in his left hand. 'On that day you shall be exposed, not one secret of yours concealed. Then as for him who is given his book in his right hand, he shall say, "Here, take and read my book! Certainly I thought that I should encounter my reckoning.". . . But as for him who is given his book in his left hand, he shall say, "Would that I had not been given my book and not known my reckoning! Would it had been the end!" ' (69:18–20,25–27) 'Neither is any diminished in his life, but it is in a Book' (35:12).

Beyond this concept of a book of reckoning, which he shared with both the Old and New Testament, Muhammad saw the book as having a very special and unique importance— as the Koran. The Koran is the book whose author is Allah, and which was dictated word by word to the Prophet by Gabriel as intermediary. Muhammad regarded the dissemination of this divine text as his duty. Later there were vigorous arguments among Islamic theologians as to whether the Koran belonged in any way to the category of created things, or whether it was just as eternal as its divine author. While it is with him, the book composed by Allah is described in the Koran as the 'Essence of the Book' *umm al kitab* (13:39), as the archetypal book. 'And behold, it is in the Essence of the Book, with Us' (43:3).

Allah's authorship is illustrated by the strange doctrine of 'abrogation', the cancellation of certain passages. An author can make as many alterations in his book as he pleases. Allah like a Sultan with absolute sovereignty can do the same. 'God blots out, and He establishes whatsoever He will' (13:39). 'And for whatever verse We abrogate or cast into oblivion, We bring a better or the like of it; knowest thou not that God is powerful over everything?' (2:100). 'We shall make you recite Our revelations, so that you shall not forget any of them except what Allah pleases [what he wants to blot out]' (87:6 Dawood).

The archetypal Koran that is with Allah occupies the same place in Islam as the Son in John's Gospel. The Son is the eternal Word, which was in the beginning with God, and was then sent down to earth. Islam's 'act of salvation' is not the descent of the Word in human form, but the sending down of the Book itself. Just as Christians celebrate Christmas, Islam celebrates the 'Night of Qadr', the night of the power of divine destiny. One night in the month of Ramadan the Koran was sent down from the heights of heaven, first of all to the lowest sphere of heaven, the realm of angels which borders the realm of man. From there Gabriel gave the book by instalments to Muhammad. The Holy Night is the subject of Sura 97.

We revealed the Koran on the Night of Qadr.

Would that you knew what the Night of Qadr is like!

Better is the Night of Qadr than a thousand months.

On that night the angels and the Spirit by their Lord's
leave come down with His decrees.

That night is peace, till break of dawn. (Dawood)

# The Book

'We swear by the Glorious Book that We revealed the Koran on a blessed night' (44:1 Dawood). 'The month of Ramadan, wherein the Koran was sent down to be a guidance to the people' (2:181). 'This is a Book which We have sent down, blessed' (6:156). Just as the birth at Christmas is associated with the Holy Spirit so is the sending down of the Koran. 'Brought down by the Faithful Spirit' (26:192). 'The Holy Spirit sent it down' (16:104). 'It is surely a noble Koran in a hidden Book none but the purified shall touch, a sending down from the Lord of all Being' (56:76–79). 'Nay, but it is a glorious Koran, in a guarded tablet' (85:21).

The Koran sent down to Gabriel's realm was not conveyed to Muhammad on one occasion but with a kind of divine pedagogy was revealed in a number of instalments over a period of twenty-two years. 'The unbelievers say, "Why has the Koran not been sent down upon him all at once?"Even so, that We may strengthen thy heart thereby, and We have chanted it very distinctly' (25:34). 'And a Koran We have divided, for thee to recite it to mankind at intervals, and We have sent it down successively' (17:107). Allah says to Muhammad: 'Even so we have revealed to thee a Spirit of Our bidding [Gabriel]. Thou knewest not what the Book was, nor belief; but We made it a light, whereby We guide whom We will of Our servants' (45:52).

Gabriel's dictation to Muhammad began with the sura numbered 96 in the Koran. This happened on a night during Ramadan on Mount Hirā. Significantly the very first word is 'Recite!' The Arab word means read and then repeat by rote. The exhortation to read is characteristic.

The sending down of the authentic text of the 'Essence of the Book' confirmed the revelations made to earlier prophets or revised them. In certain cases, as we have seen, the texts of the Jews and Christians were corrected, the texts of the Torah and the Gospel of Jesus. Jesus was considered to be merely the bearer of a book.

Muhammad regarded Christianity as a development of Judaism. The main point of the Gospel was that Jesus had brought some relaxations of the strict Mosaic Law. The Christians were for him a 'people of the book'.

It is in contrast to this belief that the act of salvation was the sending down of a book that the characteristic quality of Christianity is clearly seen. It is important that Jesus Christ himself did not write a book. On one occasion only, in the Gospel of John, is Jesus described for us as writing. When the woman taken in adultery was brought to him 'Jesus bent down and wrote with his finger on the ground' (John 8:6,8). That was not the literary writing of an author. Something was impressed upon the earth in its supersensible living essence. Goethe describes writing of this sort in a poem in the supplement to the 'Divan'. 'Drawn on the moving dust the wind blows it [the writing] away. But its power remains riveted to the ground as far as the centre of the earth.' There is also a solitary mention of Christ writing in the Apocalypse. It is the passage where the Risen Lord makes a promise to him 'who conquers': 'I will write on him the name of my God and the name of the city of my God, the new Jerusalem . . . and my own new name' (Rev.3:12). Here again it is a matter of a real pressure making an impression on a supersensible substance, which in this case is a man imbued with Christ. Otherwise the New Testament knows nothing of any writing by Christ. He can however give John on Patmos the task of writing down his living words for the churches. Himself, however, he is the Logos in person, the living Word in its divine archetype, in its archetypal divinity.

This is why he repeatedly clashes with the scribes, administrators of a book religion, who guard the mere letters without any higher inspiration. Christ demands that 'your righteousness exceeds that of the scribes and Pharisees'. He spoke 'as one who had authority, and not as their scribes' (Matt.5:20; 7:29). But he did not despise the scriptures. His attitude to them is clearly expressed in the saying: 'You search the scriptures, because you think that in them you have eternal life; and it is they [in fact] that bear witness to me; yet you refuse to come to me that you may have life' (John 5:39–40). What has been written down in the holy scriptures needs to be wakened by the living spirit. Paul, himself learned in the scriptures, could say, 'for the written code kills'; death comes to the word as it is written down. 'But the Spirit gives life' (2Cor.3:6). The Greek word for 'to read' is *ana-ginōskein*, which means literally 'to perceive in an upward direction'. The perceptive reader wakens what is lying in the grave. This is how Christ treats the holy scriptures. On the road to Emmaus the Risen Lord 'opened' the scriptures to his two companions on the road (Luke 24:32). He 'interpreted'—in the Greek *di-hermeneuein*, which contains the name of Hermes—'in all the scriptures the things concerning himself' (Luke 24:27). In the evening in the circle of the Apostles he 'opened' their 'minds', the '*nous*', the organ that can perceive the spiritual, to understand the scriptures (Luke 24:45). In his speech of farewell Christ prophesies the coming of the Paraclete, the Holy Spirit, which will bring man an extension of consciousness over and beyond everyday consciousness. In direct 'remembrance' and without external means man is to have the ability to become aware of the words then spoken by Christ (John 14:26), that is to say independent of any material book.

Christ said: 'I am with you always', not 'my book is with you always'. Although Christianity also has the inspired book, the book serves the living Logos; it is not in itself the act of salvation. For all the high estimation of the New Testament,

Christianity by its very nature is not really a book religion in the strict sense that Islam is. Reading from holy scriptures forms the first part of the Christian divine service; then follow sacrifice, transubstantiation and communion, the experience of the presence of Christ, who actually imparts himself. The divine service in a mosque stops at the first part—at the reading from the holy book.

Islam's lack of pictures is connected with the belief that the book is the real act of salvation. The ban on images which in Moses' time had been justified on grounds of divine 'pedagogy' came back again in Islam, the fact being ignored that by becoming man 'the image (*eikōn*) of the invisible God' (Col. 1:15) had appeared on earth. This gave Christianity, in the broadest sense, the opportunity for the development of art. The mosque tolerates no image at all. In Islam it is forbidden to make a copy of any living thing, even if it is only in a picture. Only Allah may do this. Pictorial art has had to restrict itself to geometrical ornament, to the arabesque and beautifully written verses from the Koran. The achievements in calligraphy, using the decorative Arabic alphabet, are superb. Islam's lack of pictures as well as the ban on music in the service was conducive to abstract thinking, and in particular the abstractions of mathematical formulae. Arab science cannot deal with form, nor the quality of a colour; it cannot give a real picture of the world.

# Ink and Pen

The earliest sura, Sura 96, opens with the command 'Recite!' and this call to recite is immediately repeated. The repeated call is followed by a mention of the Pen. 'Recite: And thy Lord is the Most Generous, who taught by the Pen, taught

Man that he knew not' (96:3–5). Sura 68 has the title *Al Qalam*, the Pen. It begins: 'By the Pen, and what they inscribe'. *Qalam* corresponds to the Greek *kalamos*, the reed. The Koran contains this strange image: 'If all the trees in the earth were pens, and the sea, with seven more seas to replenish it, were ink, the writing of Allah's words could never be finished' (31:27 Dawood). The oceans of the world are compared to ink: 'If the waters of the sea were ink with which to write the words of my Lord, the sea would surely be consumed before His words were finished, though we brought another sea to replenish it' (18:109 Dawood).

The image of the seas as ink and the trees as pens would be unthinkable in the Bible. Perhaps the final sentence of John's Gospel could be cited, which indeed was not written by John but his friends who published the Gospel after his death ('and we know that his testimony is true'). There it is said 'that the world itself could not contain the books that would be written' (John 21:25). In spite of this similarity, the passages in the Koran have a particular nuance, one that is characteristic of the type of soul and spirit that strives for intellectual attainment. There is a traditional saying of Muhammad which is not in the Koran; this is on the same lines and has the nuance that is so different from anything in the New Testament. The Prophet is said to have declared that the ink of seekers after scientific knowledge has more worth than the blood of martyrs.

Pen and ink are mentioned in the New Testament too in the Second and Third Letters of John. At the end of the Third Letter John says: 'I had much to write to you, but I would rather not write with pen and ink'. Similarly he says at the end of the Second Letter: 'Though I have much to write to you, I would rather not use paper and ink.' The Greek word he uses for paper is *chártēs*, which means a papyrus leaf. Outside China there was not yet any real paper. It is again characteristic of the nature of Arab culture that it seized on the paper which the Chinese had already learned to manufacture and with great energy brought it into use. A paper mill already existed in 794 In Baghdad: the first European paper mill was constructed in Italy in 1340. Returning to John's letters, it is to be noticed that the writer dispenses with writing at length. The writing tools which are treated with such respect in the Koran are for him only an inadequate substitute for the living word. John hopes to talk 'face to face' (2John 12; 3John 14).

In Muhammad's lifetime their great intellectual mission still lay in the future for the Arabs. They were destined to lead the era of abstract book knowledge to a high point. With untapped energy they approached this task, having been taught by the Koran to respect book, ink and pen. The sentiment the young Schiller made his Karl Moor utter would have been quite foreign to them: 'I am sick of this age of scribblers'.* A feeling was rising in him that in the long run book learning cannot be accepted as the only possible and rewarding form for man's pursuit of knowledge.

* *The Robbers*, Act I, Scene 2.

# V

# The Religious Feeling
# of the Koran

## Submission

As well as giving the initial impulse that was to lead to the
Arab culture of the future, adapting the Arab soul to its unique
character, the Koran produced one other effect. Despite the
one-sided character of its religious feeling it nevertheless created
a counterbalance to the growing and powerful intellectualism.
The cold shock to the soul which this 'greatest impulse given
to the human intellect' unavoidably brought with it was
mitigated by the advance of Islam.* Even if the contents of the
Koran and the results of the mathematical and scientific
researches of Arab culture seem to exist side by side by accident,
it was nevertheless important to the leaders of this culture and
their pupils that they lived in the religious environment of
Islam as well as in the world of scholarship.

The word 'Islam' means submission. Submission according
to the Koran was the distinguishing mark of the religion of
Abraham. 'When his Lord said to him, "Surrender," he said,
"I have surrendered me to the Lord of all Being"' (2:125).
Submission to the will of God is a basic part of all religion.
'If Islam means submission to the Will of God, all of us live and
die in Islam' said Goethe in the 'Book of Aphorisms' in his
'Divan'. But even this, common as it is to all religions, strikes
an unusual note in the Koran, because the Divine Son is not
acknowledged. The difference between Christianity and Islam
is once more clearly demonstrated.

* Rudolf Steiner, *How do I find the Christ?*

Because of its rejection of the Trinity, Islam is restricted to being a 'father religion'—and it is this in a restricted sense only, so that the word 'father' is not really applicable. The Koran knows Allah only as the Lord of All, and it is revealing that Allah is never addressed as 'Father'. The Koran not only denies him the Son but any children at all. 'God has not taken to Himself any son' (23:93; also 25:2). Submission acquires its peculiar complexion in Islam because it is prostration at a master's command which comes down to man from an external source above. This is not a father's command. It is proof of the sentence in the First Letter of John: 'No one who denies the Son has the Father. He who confesses the Son has the Father also' (1John 2:23).

Submission takes on a different character in the 'son religion' of Christianity. The great illustration of this is Gethsemane. 'Not as I will, but as thou wilt' (Matt.26:39). This must now be considered in greater detail. If the happening at Gethsemane is to be rightly understood it is first of all necessary to go further and ask what this terrible conflict was about. Until recently the opinion generally held was that Christ shrank back from death and 'lost his nerve' in the last minute, to use a modern expression. Christ therefore prayed that he might be spared the Passion, but nevertheless resigned himself to it. This interpretation contradicts a remarkable passage in the Letter to the Hebrews. Clearly based on genuine tradition it reports that 'In the days of his flesh, Jesus offered up prayers and supplications, with loud cries and tears, to him who was able to save him from death, and he was heard for his godly fear. Although he was a Son, he learned obedience through what he suffered' (5:7-8). How is the expression, 'he was heard' to be understood?

A light is thrown on this problem if we consider the description Rudolf Steiner gave from his own spiritual vision: A divine being living in an earthly body burnt up, as it were, and

consumed that body, and at the time of the Passover in the
year 33 had already brought it close to death. At the Last
Supper, Christ gave his life force to his disciples. But they
rejected it by not finding the right response to this sacrifice.
Instead of forming a protective circle round him and by their
nearness to him helping him to continue in the failing body,
they underwent a loss of awareness and abandoned him to a
final loneliness. Death tried to take him before the proper time,
before he was able to suffer the death on the cross which in all
his preaching about his sufferings he had prophetically foretold.
Until now he had moved consciously towards the death on the
cross, accepting it as belonging, in accordance with the
prophecies, to the 'rite' that should complete the Mystery of
Golgotha. But in Gethsemane his body was already in 'agony',
as Luke, the doctor, puts it (Luke 22:44). As he prayed that
death might pass him by he was in reality praying for the
strength to complete Golgotha according to the prophecies.
'The spirit . . . is willing'. He wished to celebrate the destined
event of Golgotha as the great ritual of revelation right to the
very end. He therefore rejected Peter's sword and refused to
summon the 'twelve legions of angels'. 'But how then should
the scriptures be fulfilled, that it must be so?' (Matt.26:53-54).
The urgent prayer in Gethsemane does not mean that the
willingness of the spirit was shaken. 'But the flesh is weak' —
the earthly body has reached the end of its strength. This
prayer of the willing spirit made it possible for an angel to
bring strength to the failing body. The passage in the Letter to
the Hebrews which says 'he was heard' in Gethsemane can
now be understood, and equally the obedience that the Son
then learned. To what extent?

In his death agony Christ saw the premature collapse
approaching him as something completely incomprehensible
which must thwart the divinely planned destiny as it had

always appeared to his spiritual sight. After long inner struggle he made up his mind to accept this incomprehensible collapse, if this had to be, as coming from his father: 'not as I will, but as thou wilt' (Matt.26:39); in Luke's version: 'nevertheless not my will, but thine, be done' (22:42). At this point the New Testament seems to be quite near 'submission' in the Islamic sense, going even as far as 'he fell on his face' and 'he fell on the ground' (Matt.26:39; Mark 14:35). But it is precisely in these passages that the difference becomes even more impressively clear. Christ does not resign himself fatalistically to the will of a master; he yields to the will of a father. It is a remarkable fact that nowhere else in the Gospels does Christ address his prayer to 'My father', as he does in Gethsemane (Matt.26:39,42). It is precisely here that the relationship of the Son to the Father is uniquely shown.

In the words of the Letter to the Hebrews the Son 'learned' something, and that indeed was something which he could never have learned in this way in Heaven; he could only learn it by becoming flesh in a human body doomed to die. 'The Son learned'; something new came into existence; the relationship between Father and Son was deepened by this readiness for such a last sacrifice.

The relationship even prior to this was not stationary, something fixed. A glance at John's Gospel reveals this. It presents no dogma about the relationship of the Father to the Eternal Son arrived at by systematic theological reasoning and conclusions. If John was called 'theologian', this happened in a time when there was still a visionary theology. The 'theology' of John states that the Eternal Logos was 'God' ('God' as a predicative epithet). At the end of this Gospel Thomas experienced and acknowledged this: 'My Lord and my God!' (John 20:28). This is linked with the words of the prologue: 'And the Word was God' (John 1:1). The early Church later

120

on made this intuition of John's into the dogma of homoousian, the dogma of the Son's divine nature, in opposition to the Arians, who regarded the Logos as a demigod of lower rank. The Arians cited among other things the saying in the speech of farewell: 'the Father is greater than I' (John 14:28). They misunderstood it. 'The father is greater than I'—this sentence would have a touch of blasphemy were it not for the fact that it is spoken by a being existing on a level comparable to that of God the Father, who must necessarily also himself be of divine rank. Care must be taken not abstractly to set a 'theology of subordination' against a 'theology of homoousian'. They both occur together in the Gospel of John. That the Father is greater is the basis for a relationship of the divine persons to each other which is understood to be not static but moving. Eternity is peaceful, although within it there is lively movement. In John's Gospel this is indicated by a delicate nuance of expression. 'In the beginning *was* the Word'. This is the first statement. The Word did not come into existence with the beginning, it was already there and had been for all eternity. In this word 'was' is to be found the majestic peace of eternity. In the next sentence of the prologue, 'and the Word was with God', the translation misses something of the original text. It should read, 'and the Word was towards God', for the Greek has '*pros*' with the accusative. This means a movement of approach. The contact of men living together on earth can lead, if it remains superficial, to an unproductive togetherness, for they already know each other inside and out. The relationship of the Eternal Son to the Father is not static; it is an unceasing penetration of the depths of uncreated being. The First Letter of John uses similar language: 'we . . . proclaim to you the eternal life which was with the Father and was made manifest to us' (1:2).

Similarly at the end of the prologue: 'the only Son, who is

in the bosom of the Father' (John 1:18). Here again the original text does not have 'en' followed by the dative to give 'in the bosom', which would mean a steady, persistent state. In this sense the poor Lazarus was 'in Abraham's bosom' (Luke 16:23). John uses this 'en' with the dative to describe the disciple whom Jesus loved resting on the Lord's breast, but he consciously avoids the dative in the prologue. Instead of en he uses eis, which means 'into', and is followed by the accusative. The only begotten Son is described as 'being into the soul of the Father'. The word 'being' again expresses the peacefulness of eternity, the expression 'into the soul' the dynamic. In this mobility, which shows its gradation in the Father being 'greater', lies the reason why the Son can 'learn' without prejudice to his eternal nature and why he can never finish learning to know the Father. Gethsemane was an important step in this movement. All the time it is true that 'I seek not my own will but the will of him who sent me' (John 5:30). 'My food is to do the will of him who sent me, and to accomplish his work' (John 4:34). But this truth undergoes development in what happens at Gethsemane.

Submission is brought close to Christian people when they say the Lord's Prayer: 'Thy will be done'. But it must not be overlooked that this petition has an active side. The will of God is done 'in heaven', but not with the same readiness 'on earth'. As well as receptive readiness to submit, the prayer also contains a desire that the earth may be conquered for the coming of the kingdom of God, and that man may prove worthy of serving the realization of God's will. The true kindred of Christ are those who do 'the will of my Father in heaven' (Matt.12:50).

Christian submission does not have the fatalistic nuance characteristic of Islam and which is clearly expressed in the concept of 'a fixed decree' (54:49 Dawood). Christian submission, even to something incomprehensible, rests on the basic conviction that in the end it is a matter of submission to a father's will, a loving will.

# The Practice of Prayer

Islam develops great strength by adhering strictly to a practice of prayer. Five times a day—in the morning, at midday, late in the afternoon, in the evening and at night—the pious man spreads his prayer mat. Originally three obligatory times of prayer were laid down in the Koran—morning, midday and evening.

A custom of this sort had developed long before among both Jews and Christians. These times were based on certain very real experiences which must first of all be considered. Theoretically it must be possible to pray at any hour. In practice there is a realization that no hour of the day is like another, that certain times of the day are especially suitable for prayer. This is particularly true of the change from night to day and from day to night, and the turning points of noon and midnight. It is no accident that the appearances of the Risen Christ took place in the morning and in the evening, and that after the Fall Adam heard God's voice in the evening. It is revealing just to consider the passages in the Bible that deal with supersensible experiences simply with regard to the element of time.

In Psalm 55 we find prayer three times a day, 'evening and morning and at noon' (55:17). Psalm 32 does not speak of a 'prayer . . . at a time of distress', as the Revised Standard Version has it, but of prayer 'at a time of finding' (32:6). What is meant is a time which has proved right in the personal religious experience of the pious (*hasid* in the original text), a

time when the divine is more easily 'found' by the man seeking
God. In this way the hour of prayer can also become the golden
hour of a special blessing. 'My prayer is to Thee, O LORD. At
an acceptable time' (69:13), at the time of divine 'pleasure'.
The long Psalm 119 must clearly have had its origin in a sect
which practised a particularly strict religious discipline, one
which went further than the ritual of prayer three times a day.
'Seven times a day I praise thee' (119:164). Christianity readily
adopted the practice of praying three times a day. The didache,
the early Christian 'Teaching of the twelve Apostles', gives the
text of the Lord's Prayer and ordains: 'Three times a day you
are to pray in this way'.

Allah speaks in the same way in the Koran. 'Prayer is a duty
incumbent on the faithful, to be conducted at appointed hours'
(4:103 Dawood). As a child of nature Muhammad had a vivid
religious feeling for the change from day to night. 'Surely in
the creation of the heavens and earth and in the alternation of
night and day there are signs for men possessed of minds'
3:187). It is more than poetic feeling when Sura 81 calls as
witnesses 'the night swarming' and 'the dawn sighing' (81:17,
18). 'Say: "Think! If Allah should enshroud you in perpetual
night till the Day of Resurrection, what other god could give
you light? Have you no ears to hear with?" Say: "Think! If
Allah should give perpetual day until the Resurrection, what
other god could bring you the night to sleep in? Have you no
eyes to see with?" In His mercy He has given you the night
that you may rest in it, and the day that you may seek His
bounty and render thanks' (28:71–73 Dawood). The long
shadows in the morning and evening are in the Koran images
of creation prostrating itself before the majesty of Allah. 'To
God bow all who are in the heavens and the earth . . . as do
their shadows also in the mornings and the evenings' (13:15).

The holiness of the night was deeply felt. There was still an ancient knowledge that sleep did not have only a biological importance. The soul abandons the experience of the organs of sense and enters a supersensible world. This is wonderfully expressed in the Koran. 'With Him are the keys of the Unseen; none knows them but He. He knows what is in land and sea; not a leaf falls, but He knows it. Not a grain in the earth's shadows, not a thing, fresh or withered, but it is in a Book Manifest. It is He who recalls you by night, and He knows what you work by day; then He raises you up . . .' (6:59,60). In death this 'recalls you' becomes final. 'God takes the souls at the time of their death, and that which has not died, in its sleep; He withholds that against which He has decreed death, but looses the other till a stated term' (39:43).

Anyone waking up in the night experiences something of the mystery of night. He does not, although sleepless, continue with the ordinary daytime consciousness into the hours of night, but feels how very near the supersensible world is. 'If thou triest my heart, if thou visitest me by night, if thou testest me . . .' (Ps.17:3). The historian Ammianus Marcellinus wrote in the fourth century that the Emperor Julian had a mortal wound and died 'in the horror of the night' (*medio horrore noctis*). In this 'horror' the last echoes of primal visionary experience can be heard, visionary experience which could overwhelm the soul with intimations of another world. In this way the hours of night create a special inclination to pray. In addition to the obligatory times of prayer, the last of which is at the onset of darkness, there is also for the pious a real prayer of the night which is an additional, voluntary exercise. This occupies an important place in the Koran. Here again Muhammad can find a connection with Judaism and Christianity. 'At midnight I rise to praise thee . . .' (Ps.119:62). The righteous man has 'his delight in the law of the LORD and on his law he meditates [*hagah*] day and night' (Ps.1:2). Psalm 134

125

was sung at a night time ceremony: 'Come, bless the LORD, all you servants of the LORD, who stand by night in the house of the LORD!' Before appointing the twelve Apostles Christ spent the night on the mountain praying to God (Luke 6:12). Paul and Silas prayed at midnight in the prison at Philippi (Acts 16:25). Muhammad knew about the practice of nightly prayers in the Christian communities. 'Some of the People of the Book are a nation upstanding, that recite God's signs in the watches of the night, bowing themselves' (3:109).

The prayer at night is particularly important in the early suras of the Mecca period. In Medina everything was much more 'established', and detailed rules concerning the times for prayer were laid down for the faithful. The enthusiasm of the first Mecca years, which was still untroubled by a possible overburdening of the faithful, is no longer in such evidence in the Medina suras. Almost all the references to prayer at night belong to the Mecca period. The early Sura 73 has: 'It is in the watches of the night that impressions are strongest and words most eloquent; in the day-time you are hard-pressed with work. Remember the name of your Lord and dedicate yourself to Him utterly . . . your Lord knows that you [Muhammad] sometimes keep vigil nearly two-thirds of the night and sometimes half or one-third of it, as do others among your followers. Allah measures the night and the day' (73:6–8,20 Dawood). 'And remember the Name of thy Lord at dawn and in the evening and part of the night; bow down before Him and magnify Him through the long night' (76:25,26). 'Proclaim the praise of thy Lord when thou arisest, and proclaim the praise of thy Lord in the night, and at the declining of the stars' (52:48,49). 'Surely the godfearing shall be among gardens and fountains [of Paradise] . . . Little of the night would they slumber, and in the mornings they would ask for forgiveness' (51:15–18). 'Proclaim thy Lord's praise before the rising of the

126

sun, and before its setting, and proclaim thy Lord's praise in the night' (50:38-39). 'Or is he who is obedient in the watches of the night, bowing himself and standing, he being afraid of the world to come and hoping for the mercy of his Lord?' (39:12). 'The servants of the All-merciful are those who walk in the earth modestly and who, when the ignorant address them, say, "Peace"; who pass the night prostrate to their Lord and standing' (25:64). 'So be thou patient under what they say, and proclaim thy Lord's praise before the rising of the sun, and before its setting, and proclaim thy Lord's praise in the watches of the night, and at the ends of the day; haply thou wilt be well-pleasing ... And bid thy family to pray, and be thou patient in it' (20:130,132). 'Recite your prayers at sunset, at nightfall, and at dawn; the dawn prayer has its witnesses. Pray during the night as well, an additional duty for the fulfilment of which your Lord may exalt you to an honourable station. Say: "Lord grant me a goodly entrance and a goodly exit" ' (17:80-82 Dawood). The last sentence echoes verse 8 of Psalm 121.

The prayers are based on recitation of the Koran and their character is that of praise and worship. A mood of prostrate awe is constantly sustained in the Koran by the description of Allah as the All-powerful Lord of the universe who graciously reveals himself in nature's gifts. This is a continuation of what is already present in the Old Testament. 'He is the First and the Last' (57:3). This takes up Isaiah's prophecy (Isa.44:6; 48:12) which had meanwhile been further developed in the Apocalypse (Rev.1:17; 2:8; 22:13). The Koran adds 'the Outward and the Inward' (57:3). Much quoted and used on amulets is the so-called Throne Verse, one of the most sublime hymns in the Koran. 'God there is no God but He, the Living, the Everlasting. Slumber seizes Him not, neither sleep; to Him belongs all that is in the heavens and the earth. Who is there that shall intercede with Him save by His leave? He knows what lies before them and what is after them, and they comprehend not anything of His knowledge save such as He wills. His Throne comprises the heavens and earth; the preserving of them oppresses Him not; He is the All-high, the All-glorious' (2:256). One cannot fail to bear echoes of the Old Testament: 'Behold, he who keeps Israel will neither slumber nor sleep' (Ps.121:4); 'Heaven is my throne and the earth is my footstool' (Isa.66:1); 'For all that is in the heavens and in the earth is thine' (Prayer of David, 1Chron.29:11). God's universal presence is expressed in Psalm 139, and this is described in the Koran with a strangely powerful image: 'We indeed created man; and We know what his soul whispers within him, and We are nearer to him than the jugular vein' (50:15). This near presence is contrasted with Allah's universal extent: 'Surely My earth is wide; therefore Me do you serve!' (29:56). 'God holds the heavens and the earth, lest they remove; did they remove, none would hold them after Him' (35:39).

The repeated offering of worship and adoration has a pacifying influence on the soul. 'He guides . . . those who believe, their hearts being at rest in God's remembrance—in God's remembrance are at rest the hearts of those who believe' (13:28). At prayer man is freed from dependence on the outer world. 'Decked out fair to men is the love of lusts—women, children, heaped-up heaps of gold and silver, horses of mark, cattle and tillage. That is the enjoyment of the present life; but God—with Him is the fairest resort' (3:12). 'All things perish, except His Face' (28:88). Whoever has 'sent on ahead' his thoughts and feelings in prayer to the hereafter can confidently attend the Last Judgment. 'O soul at peace, return unto thy Lord, well-pleased, well-pleasing! Enter thou among My servants! Enter thou My Paradise!' (89:27–30).

Although Muhammad may have had many human failings,

there can be no doubt about the sincerity and piety of his prayers. Prayer was for him something resembling a bridge to a God whose majesty made him approachable in no other way. In Sura 22 rules for sacrifices are given. 'We have made the camels a part of Allah's rites. They are of much use to you. Pronounce over them the name of Allah as you draw them up in line and slaughter them; and when they have fallen down eat of their flesh and feed with it the poor man and the beggar. Thus We have subjected them to your service, so that you may give thanks. Their flesh and blood does not reach Allah; it is your piety that reaches Him' (22:38 Dawood).

The worship practised by Islam is a sublime religious achievement. But it does have a one-sided character. The God is worshipped who has no 'companions' and 'associates' and who has no one of his own kind with him. In agreement with the Old Testament—'You shall have no other gods before me' (Ex.20:3)—Muhammad always continued to combat the sin of 'giving companions to God'. Christianity, however, took a step forward, not a step backward. God is revealed as Love, and because of this Love seeks to share his divinity. This took place in eternity with the Son, but is to be continued with mankind. As a result of this loving desire to share, God seeks 'companions' and 'associates', and in the First Letter to the Corinthians there is an expression which in the Koran would be utterly unthinkable: 'For we are God's fellow workers [*synergoi*]' (3:9). When this summons to be a fellow worker dawns on man his worship develops a new dimension, a dimension that is lacking as long as worship is only prostration before an overwhelming omnipotence.

# VI
# The Shiah
# another form of Islam

## Muhammad's View of Himself

A description of the further development of Islam does not
fall within the scope of this work. It is permissible, however,
briefly to review the singular development that Islam underwent in Persia, and that reveals a definite feeling that the
religion of Muhammad had inadequacies. Muhammad could
rank Jesus only as a prophet, albeit a particularly important
one, who, like the other prophets, as a messenger of joy and
warning had to transmit his 'book'. He had been overtaken,
however, by Muhammad who as 'Seal of the Prophets'
(Sura 33:40) completes the line of prophets, crowning it in a
way that cannot be surpassed. Muhammad applied to himself
Christ's prophecy of the Counsellor, the Paraclete, who would
come after him (John 14:16–17,26; 15:26; 16:7–14). 'Jesus son
of Mary said, "Children of Israel, I am indeed the Messenger
of God to you, confirming the Torah that is before me, and
giving good tidings of a Messenger who shall come after me,
whose name shall be Ahmad." ' (61:6). 'Ahmad' means 'he
who is longed for' which is more or less a rendering of the
word *Paraclete*, which means 'he who is summoned'.

Muhammad knows himself to be *the* Prophet and *the*
Messenger of God. Alongside this very considerable self-
confidence there was also a certain metaphysical humility,
imposed on him by his conception of God as strictly exclusive.
There was an impassable barrier between Allah and his creature,

man. So Muhammad resigned himself to the limits of his mortality, of his being a creature, a man.

'Muhammad is naught but a Messenger; Messengers have passed away before him. Why, if he should die or is slain, will you turn about on your heels? [lose courage] . . . It is not given to any soul to die, save by the leave of God, at an appointed time' (3:138). The events in Medina after his death on June 8, 632 show that such a declaration of his 'non-immortality' was not uncalled-for. Many people were unwilling to believe that he was dead. Perhaps he was only lost in a trance? The passionate Umar even drew his sword and swore he would cut off the hands and feet of anyone who said that Muhammad was dead.★ Level-headed old Abu Bakr calmed him with great difficulty and pointed out the Prophet's own words. There are other passages expressing this attitude.

Say: 'I do not say to you, "I possess the treasuries of God"; I know not the Unseen. And I say not to you, "I am an angel"; I only follow what is revealed to me' (6:50).

They say, 'Why has a sign not been sent down upon him from his Lord?' Say: 'The Unseen belongs only to God. Then watch and wait; I shall be with you watching and waiting' (10:21).

They say: 'We will not believe thee till thou makest a spring to gush forth from the earth for us, or till thou possessest a garden of palms and vines, and thou makest rivers to gush forth abundantly all amongst it, or till thou makest heaven to fall, as thou assertest, on us in fragments, or thou bringest God and the angels as a surety, or till thou possessest a house of gold ornament, or till thou goest up into heaven; and we will not believe thy going up till thou bringest down on us a book that we may read.' Say:

★ Washington Irving, *Mahomet and his Successors*, p. 186.

'Glory be to my Lord! Am I aught but a mortal, a Messenger?' (17:92–95).

Say: 'I am only a mortal the like of you; it is revealed to me that your God is One God' (18:110; also 41:5).

They also say, 'What ails this Messenger that he eats food, and goes in the markets? Why has an angel not been sent down to him, to be a warner with him? Or why is not a treasure thrown to him, or why has he not a Garden to eat of?' (25:8,9).

# Ali

Because of a feeling of 'metaphysical inadequacy' and religious insufficiency eyes were turned in the direction of one who belonged to the Prophet's intimate circle. This was Ali, a cousin of Muhammad, who had married his favourite daughter Fātima, a daughter of Khadija. Muhammad had no son himself, but Fātima bore Ali two sons, Hasan and Husayn, Muhammad's grandchildren. Only through them had Muhammad any descendants.

Ali had been greatly attached to the Prophet from the beginning. According to everything that has come down to us he must have been a distinguished and sympathetic person, a brave, generous and noble character. When the Prophet died, old Abu Bakr was first of all chosen as his successor. He ruled successfully for two years. Ali took it badly that he had been passed over; and this happened again on two occasions. When Abu Bakr died in 634, Umar was chosen—a powerful, straightforward man and a great soldier. He it was who entered Jerusalem in 638 and who conquered the new Persian Empire of the Sassanids. In 644 he was murdered by a Persian prisoner. Once more Ali had to stand back as Uthmān was

chosen, who belonged to the Quraysh family of the
Umayyads. Uthmān, who had prepared a standard revised
edition of the Koran, was murdered in 656 while reading the
Koran. At last Ali was considered, a man who had been so
close to the Prophet. Now at last he was chosen caliph, but this
brought him little joy. The Umayyad Muāwiya contested the
choice. War broke out. Ali was winning when Muāwiya
snatched certain victory out of his hands by means of a shabby
trick. He made his soldiers fix the Koran to their lances and
Ali's troops would not tackle them, so much did they respect
the Holy Book. Ali lost his chance. In 661 he was murdered
in the mosque at Kūfa in Iraq. As he lay dying he still managed
to give an order that the murderer was not to be tortured but
executed with *one* stroke. The thirty-six-year-old man had
already had premonitions of death, and was subject to fits of
melancholy—'life is only the shadow of a cloud, a sleeper's
dream.' Muāwiya was now caliph. Contrary to the previous
practice of choosing a successor he founded an hereditary
caliphate of the Umayyad family, with its seat at Damascus.
After Ali's death, his son Hasan was an obstacle. His followers
claimed that he was his father's successor. But Hasan was not
war-like and wanted a quiet, withdrawn life. He made an agreement with Muāwiya; he recognized Muāwiya as caliph and in
return retired with a pension from him. One of Hasan's wives
was a Persian princess, the daughter of the last Persian king.
Although he was politically harmless Hasan was poisoned in
669. Dying, he refused to give the name of the murderer—
'this world is only a long night, leave the murderer in peace;
I shall meet him in the bright light of day, in the presence of
the All-highest.'

His brother Husayn was more active and belligerent. He
found himself confronted after Muāwiya's death by his son and
successor, Yazid. He carelessly accepted an invitation and went

133

with his supporters to Kūfa, but before reaching Kūfa he found himself and his small band of supporters surrounded by Yazid's army at Karbala. Like his father and his brother he too suffered from a melancholy obsession with death. After fighting bravely and spending the night in prayer he yielded to superior force. He was beheaded and the head brought to Yazid at Damascus. This was in 680. This bloody end of Muhammad's descendants aroused strong feelings. Ali's supporters formed the 'Shiah', meaning the 'Party', that is to say the party of Ali. Towards the end of the seventh century the Shiah was strongly supported, above all in Persia. From it arose a kind of Ali-mysticism.

# The Imam

The line of Ali, Hasan and Husayn was continued by Husayn's son Ali. Each successor and heir by blood was recognized by supporters, even if there could be no question of a publicly acknowledged caliphate. The ruling Umayyads, and after them the Abbāsids, kept Ali's successors under strict control. They had quietly to turn their attention to the life of the spirit.

They were given the name of 'imam'. This is a word which can be applied to any head of a religious organization; it can also be applied, though in a special sense, to a religious leader. In the language of the Shiah it acquired great distinction.

The imams of Ali's line were clearly men of spiritual importance. The Shiah preserved their sayings in comprehensive records. There developed the idea of a whole spiritual world of a gnostic mystical character, a kind of theosophy, which was especially cultivated in Persia and went far beyond Islam proper. Ali had spoken of his close relationship to Muhammad: 'No verse of the Koran came down to God's Messenger without his

The Imam

dictating it to me and making me recite it. I copied it out with
my own hand. He taught me the literal meaning and the
spiritual interpretation. He prayed to Allah to increase my
understanding and memory. Then he placed his hand on my
breast and prayed to Allah to fill my heart with knowledge
and understanding, with judgment and with light.'* Muhammad had brought the actual text of the Koran, but it was in
Ali that the Koran now found its esoteric interpreter. The line
of prophets had finally ended with Muhammad. It was accepted
as an immutable fact that the time for founding a public
religion and a law-giving control had ended with the 'Seal of
the Prophets'. But by the side of the last of the prophets there
appeared the first of the 'imams', of the intimate and esoteric
spiritual teachers. In this way the one-sidedness of a religion
that looked only to the past was counteracted, and a way to
further development opened.

Ali is the first but not the only imam. There was seen working in him a pre-existing 'light-substance' which came from
eternity, and this was inherited in spiritual succession by his
heirs. These successors were all descended through Fātima from
Muhammad, and so his blood continued to flow in their veins.
The objection that this physical inheritance could be other than
spiritual was countered by the argument that the imams in
question had been spiritually related before their life on earth
and this already existing spiritual relationship was merely
reflected by their blood relationship. In fact quite a number of
distinguished personalities succeeded each other in the line of
imams—a line of twelve imams. The line ceased with the
twelfth imam. The eleventh had married a Byzantine
princess, and was held in Samara under police supervision by
the Abbāsid caliph, who now lived in Baghdad. The imam
died in 873 when he was 28. The imam's light-substance

* Henri Corbin, *Histoire de la philosophie islamique*, p. 72.

passed therefore to his eldest son; but he was a five-year-old child—and he disappeared without trace on the day of his father's death. From a secret and hidden place the twelfth imam still managed to establish occasional contact with his supporters by means of go-betweens for a period of seventy years. After that this 'Little Concealment' changed in 942 to the 'Great Concealment'. The twelfth imam became the 'Hidden Imam', whose real but supersensible, invisible and mysterious presence can be sensed in the organ of the heart. Only when time ends will he emerge from concealment. Until then, however, he is the 'imam of this our time', the invisibly real and intimate spiritual guide who can be found in a heart that is awake.

In this way the rigid and backward-looking restriction to the literal text of the Koran is largely overcome for the benefit of future development.

Ali's supporters formed the 'Shiah', the 'Party', the Party of Ali. In 1502 the Shiah became the established religion of Persia. By the rest of Islam it was regarded as heresy. The 'Hidden Imam' is not just the dogma of a sect. As Corbin reports, there is evidence of numerous religious experiences of which his mysterious presence was the content. He can be seen in dreams. The reverent turning to the 'Hidden Imam' in the heart opens up the possibility of an encounter with the Christ, who is ever near to mankind, even though the experience might be called differently.

Some astonishing sayings are attributed to the first imam, through whom the Eternal Imam speaks and who then works throughout the *plērōma* of the Twelve. 'I am the sign of the Almighty. I am the gnosis of the mysteries. I am the threshhold of threshholds . . . I am the first and the last, the visible and the invisible. I am the countenance of God. I am the mirror of God (p. 76*). 'Whoever has seen me has seen God' (p. 90*).

* Henri Corbin, *Histoire de la philosophie islamique*.

# The Imam

Words like this would be utterly unthinkable in the Koran. The fifth imam declared: 'The light of the Imam in the believers' hearts is brighter than the light of the sun' (p. 76*). The following words are attributed to the sixth imam: 'The human form is the highest proof of God in his creation. It is the book he has written with his own hand. It is the temple he built with his wisdom, the meeting place of all the forms in the whole universe. It is the effective proof against all negation' (p. 65*).

The Shiah developed an entire imamology, or perhaps imamosophy is the better expression. In this, statements are often made which border on Christian statements about the eternal Logos, and which go far beyond Muhammad's Koran.

Another branch is formed by the 'Shiah of Seven', which with the seventh imam went over to another line of succession. The theosophy of the 'Seven' is bolder still than that of the 'Twelve', and makes the imam markedly superior to Muhammad. 'Whoever knows himself, knows his Lord; that is, he knows his imam' (p. 145*).

In this way the Shiah developed in a remarkable spiritual direction and although it quite certainly wished to be Islamic and not Christian, nevertheless in its esoteric striving it came close to the Christian mysteries. That such a development was possible at all is proof of the very decided shortcoming of Muhammad's Islam: the uncomprehending neglect of the mystery of the Son and his becoming Man. As a result of this feeling of inadequacy, the Shiah was led along its unusual path through the veneration of Ali to the striving for the 'Hidden Imam'.

The study of Islam and its Shiah branches could give Christians the impetus to ponder anew the basic facts of Christianity and understand more profoundly John's words (1John 5:12) 'He who has the Son has life'.

* Henri Corbin, *Histoire de la philosophie islamique*.

# Bibliography

Arberry, Arthur J., *The Koran Interpreted*, Allen & Unwin, London 1955

Bethman, Erich, *Bridge to Islam*, Allen & Unwin, London 1953

Bock, Emil, *Urgeschichte* [Genesis], Urachhaus, Stuttgart 1934

Buhl, Frants, *Das Leben Muhammeds* [the life of Muhammad], Leipzig 1930; Quelle & Meyer, Heidelberg 1955

Clemen, Carl, *Die nichtchristlichen Kulturreligionen* [the non-Christian religions], Leipzig and Berlin 1920

Corbin, Henri, *Histoire de la philosophie islamique* [history of Islamic philosophy], Gallimard, Paris 1964

Dawood, N.J., *The Koran*, Penguin Classics, Harmondsworth, fourth edition 1974

Dermenghem, Emile, *Mohammed in Selbstzeugnissen und Bild-Dokumenten*, Rowohlt, Reinbeck 1960 (Translated from *Mahomet et la tradition islamique*, Seuil, Paris 1955; English: *Muhammad and the Islamic Tradition*, Longman, London, and Harper & Bros., New York 1958)

Gleich, Sigismund von, *Geisteswissenschaftliche Entwickelunslinien im Hinblick auf den Impuls von »Gondi-Schapur«* [directions of spiritual development with reference to the impulse of 'Gondi-Shapur'], Mellinger, Stuttgart 1966

Horten, M., *Die philosophischen Systeme der spekulativen Theologie im Islam* [philosophical systems of speculative theology in Islam], Bonn 1902

Hunke, Sigrid, *Allahs Sonne über dem Abendland – Unser arabisches Erbe* [Allah's sun over the west – our Arabic heritage], Deutsche Verlags-Anstalt, Stuttgart 1960

Irving, Washington, *Mahomet and his Successors*, London 1850; University of Wisconsin Press 1970

Nöldecke, Theodor, *Geschichte des Korans* [history of the Koran], Göttingen 1860

North, C.R., *An Outline of Islâm*, Epworth, London 1952

Paret, Rudi, *Mohammed und der Koran* [Muhammad and the Koran], Kohlhammer, Stuttgart 1957

Pickthall, Mohammed Marmaduke, *The Meaning of the Glorious Koran. An Explanatory Translation*, Allen & Unwin, London, and Mentor Books (New American Library), New York 1953

# Bibliography

Rad, Gerhard von, *Das erste Buch Mose*, Vandenhoeck & Ruprecht, Göttingen 1956, 1961; (English: *Genesis*, SCM, London 1961, 1972)

Richter, Gottfried, '*Von der Geburt Jesu Christi*' [about the birth of Jesus Christ], *Die Christengemeinschaft*, Stuttgart, November/December 1949

——'*Von der Menschwerdung Christi*' [about Christ's becoming man], *Die Christengemeinschaft*, Stuttgart, January 1965

Rudolph, Wilhelm, *Die Abhängigkeit des Korans vom Judentum und Christentum* [the dependence of the Koran on Judaism and Christianity], Berlin and Leipzig 1922

Schütze, Alfred, *Vom Wesen der Trinität* [the essence of the Trinity], Urachhaus, Stuttgart 1954

Sarwar, Hafiz Ghulam, *Philosophy of the Quran*, Ashraf, Lahore 1955

Steiner, Rudolf, *Die Geheimwissenschaft im Umriss*, (Gesamtausgabe 13), Rudolf Steiner Verlag, Dornach 1977; (English: *Occult Science – an Outline*, Rudolf Steiner Press, London 1963)

——Lectures: March 13, 1911, *Exkurse in das Gebiet des Markus-Evangeliums*, (GA 124); (*Background to the Gospel of St. Mark*, RSP, London 1968)

——October 11 and 12, 1918, *Drei Strömungen der Menschheitsentwickelung*, (GA 184); (*Three Streams in the Evolution of Mankind*, RSP, London 1965)

——October 16, 1918, *Wie finde ich den Christus?* (GA 182); (*How do I find the Christ?*, Anthroposophic Press, New York 1941)

——March 16 and April 16, 1924, *Karma-Vorträge*, vol. I (GA 235); (*Karmic Relationships*, vol. I, RSP, London 1972)

——April 6, 1924, *Karma-Vorträge*, vol. II (GA 236), (*Karmic Relationships*, vol. II, RSP, London 1974)

——July 1 and August 1, 1924, *Karma-Vorträge*, vol. III (GA 237); (*Karmic Relationships*, vol. III, RSP, London 1977)

——September 1, 1924, *Karma-Vorträge*, vol. IV (GA 238); (*Karmic Relationships*, vol. IV, RSP, London 1957)

——March 31, April 5 and June 12, 1924, *Karma-Vorträge*, vol. V (GA 239), (*Karmic Relationships*, vol. V, RSP, London 1966)

——July 19 and August 14, 1924, *Karma-Vorträge*, vol. VI (GA 240), (*Karmic Relationships*, vol. VI, RSP, London 1971)

Tiele-Söderblom, *Kompendium der Religionsgeschichte* [compendium of the history of religion], Berlin 1920

Tritton, Arthur Stanley, *Muslim Theology*, Luzac, London 1947

——*Islam, Belief and Practices*, Hutchinson, London 1957

# Index

# Index

141

# Index